E M D R

A Practical Guide for Healing P T S D, Anxiety, and Emotional Wounds

Dr. Natalie Anderson

Table of Contents

Introduction

Healing Through E M D R – A Journey to Recovery

Every human being carries a story—some of joy, love, and growth, while others are marked by pain, fear, and unresolved wounds. These difficult chapters in our lives often leave behind scars invisible to the eye but deeply felt in the heart and mind. Trauma, anxiety, and emotional distress have a way of shaping our lives, influencing how we see ourselves, relate to others, and navigate the world around us.

But what if there was a way to rewrite the narrative? A way to confront the pain, resolve the wounds, and emerge stronger, freer, and more whole? Eye Movement Desensitization and Reprocessing (E M D R) therapy offers exactly that—a proven path to healing that empowers individuals to process their past and reclaim their present.

What This Book Is About

This book, *"E M D R: A Practical Guide for Healing P T S D, Anxiety, and Emotional Wounds,"* is a comprehensive and approachable resource designed to help you understand and harness the transformative power of E M D R therapy. Whether you're someone seeking personal healing, a caregiver supporting a loved one, or a mental health professional exploring new tools, this book will serve as your guide.

Through step-by-step instructions, real-life examples, and actionable techniques, we will explore how E M D R works and why it has become one of the most effective therapies for trauma recovery. Unlike traditional talk therapy, which often focuses on analyzing and discussing pain, E M D R goes deeper, unlocking the brain's natural healing processes to resolve the root causes of suffering.

Why E M D R?

In 1987, Dr. Francine Shapiro, the founder of E M D R, discovered that specific eye movements could help individuals process distressing memories more effectively. Over the decades, E M D R has grown into a globally recognized therapy, backed by extensive scientific research and used by mental health professionals worldwide. It is recommended by organizations like the World Health Organization (WHO) and the American Psychiatric Association (APA) as a gold standard for treating trauma and P T S D.

What sets E M D R apart is its holistic approach. It doesn't just address symptoms—it targets the core experiences that fuel anxiety, depression, and emotional distress. The result? A profound and lasting sense of relief and empowerment.

Who Is This Book For?

You don't have to be a mental health expert to benefit from this book. It is written for anyone who:

- Struggles with lingering effects of trauma, anxiety, or stress.
- Feels trapped in negative thought patterns or emotional overwhelm.
- Seeks practical tools to support healing, personal growth, or resilience.
- Wants to understand E M D R better, whether for themselves or a loved one.
- Desires to integrate E M D R techniques into their professional practice.

No matter where you are on your journey, this book meets you where you are—offering knowledge, hope, and actionable strategies to help you take the next step.

What You'll Gain

In these pages, you will:

- Learn the science behind E M D R and why it works.
- Discover practical exercises you can use to manage anxiety and emotional stress.
- Understand the eight-phase process of E M D R therapy and how it can transform your life.
- Explore self-help techniques based on E M D R principles to address everyday challenges.
- Find inspiration and motivation through real-life success stories.
- Access tools and resources to enhance your healing journey, including worksheets and guided practices.

A Journey of Transformation

Healing is not a linear path; it's a journey with twists, turns, and moments of revelation. E M D R is not a magic wand, but it is a powerful tool—a key to unlocking the door to a healthier, happier, and more resilient you.

Through this book, you will discover that healing is possible. Trauma does not define you, and your past does not have to dictate your future. With E M D R, you can process the pain, let go of the emotional weight you've been carrying, and make space for joy, peace, and fulfillment.

Welcome to the beginning of your transformation. Whether you're taking your first steps or looking to deepen your understanding, this guide will walk alongside you every step of the way.

Let's start this journey together.

Chapter 1: Understanding Trauma and Emotional Wounds

Trauma is a universal experience, yet it manifests uniquely in each individual. It can be as fleeting as a single terrifying moment or as complex as years of ongoing adversity. But no matter its form, trauma leaves a lasting imprint on the mind and body, shaping how we perceive the world, interact with others, and even understand ourselves.

In this chapter, we delve into the concept of trauma and emotional wounds, exploring their origins, effects, and the hope for healing. By understanding the nature of trauma, we take the first step toward reclaiming our lives and breaking free from its grip.

What Is Trauma?

At its core, trauma is the response to a deeply distressing or disturbing event that overwhelms an individual's ability to cope. It's not just the event itself but how our mind and body process and store the experience. Trauma disrupts our sense of safety, control, and trust, leaving us feeling vulnerable and exposed.

Types of Trauma

Trauma can be categorized into three primary types:

1. **Acute Trauma**: Results from a single, isolated event, such as an accident, natural disaster, or assault.
2. **Chronic Trauma**: Stems from prolonged exposure to distressing situations, such as abuse, neglect, or living in a war zone.
3. **Complex Trauma**: Arises from repeated, severe interpersonal trauma, often beginning in childhood, such as ongoing abuse or abandonment.

Emotional Wounds

Emotional wounds are the lingering effects of trauma. These are the "invisible scars" left behind by painful experiences, often manifesting as fear, shame, anger, or sadness. While physical injuries heal with time, emotional wounds can persist indefinitely unless actively addressed.

The Science Behind Trauma

Trauma doesn't just exist in our memories—it is stored in the brain and body. Understanding how this happens is crucial for grasping why certain symptoms arise.

The Brain's Response to Trauma

1. **Amygdala**: The brain's alarm system. During trauma, it becomes hyperactive, heightening fear and anxiety.
2. **Hippocampus**: Responsible for processing and storing memories. Trauma disrupts this process, causing fragmented, intrusive memories.
3. **Prefrontal Cortex**: The rational, decision-making part of the brain. Trauma can impair its function, making it harder to regulate emotions and think logically.

The Body Remembers

As trauma researcher Dr. Bessel van der Kolk famously said, "The body keeps the score." Trauma isn't just a mental experience; it's also physical. The nervous system can remain in a state of hyperarousal or shutdown, leading to symptoms such as:

- Increased heart rate or palpitations.
- Digestive issues and chronic pain.
- Fatigue and sleep disturbances.

Common Symptoms of Trauma and Emotional Wounds

Trauma manifests differently in each person, but some common symptoms include:

- **Emotional Symptoms**: Anxiety, depression, irritability, guilt, shame, or emotional numbness.
- **Cognitive Symptoms**: Intrusive thoughts, flashbacks, memory problems, or difficulty concentrating.
- **Behavioral Symptoms**: Avoidance of certain places or people, substance abuse, or self-isolation.
- **Physical Symptoms**: Headaches, muscle tension, or chronic illnesses.

Trauma Triggers

Triggers are reminders of the traumatic event that cause the individual to relive the experience. They can be:

- **External**: Sights, sounds, or smells resembling the traumatic event.
- **Internal**: Thoughts, emotions, or physical sensations that mimic aspects of the trauma.

Understanding your triggers is an essential part of managing trauma. By recognizing what sets off these reactions, you can begin to develop coping mechanisms.

The Ripple Effects of Trauma

Trauma doesn't just affect the individual; its impact often spreads into relationships, careers, and overall well-being.

On Relationships

- Difficulty trusting others.
- Struggles with emotional intimacy.

- Patterns of avoidance or conflict.

On Mental Health

- Increased risk of developing P T S D, anxiety disorders, or depression.
- Self-esteem issues stemming from feelings of shame or guilt.

On Physical Health

- Higher likelihood of chronic conditions, such as heart disease or autoimmune disorders, due to prolonged stress responses.

Hope for Healing

While trauma can feel insurmountable, healing is possible. The human brain and body are remarkably resilient, capable of rewiring and repairing themselves when given the right tools and support.

The Role of E M D R in Healing Trauma

E M D R offers hope by addressing the root cause of emotional wounds, allowing individuals to process distressing memories in a safe and structured way. Unlike traditional therapies, which often involve retelling the traumatic event, E M D R focuses on reprocessing the memory, reducing its emotional intensity and impact.

Other Paths to Healing

- **Therapeutic Support**: From talk therapy to group counseling, professional guidance is invaluable.
- **Mind-Body Practices**: Yoga, mindfulness, and meditation can help calm the nervous system.

- **Self-Compassion**: Healing begins with kindness toward oneself. Recognizing that trauma is not your fault is a powerful first step.

Understanding P T S D, Anxiety, and Emotional Trauma: A Practical Guide

The terms **P T S D**, **anxiety**, and **emotional trauma** are often used interchangeably, yet they describe distinct challenges that millions of people face daily. While they may overlap, each has unique characteristics that impact the mind, body, and overall well-being. In this section, readers will gain an approachable, clear understanding of these conditions, supported by relatable examples that bring the concepts to life.

What Is P T S D?

Post-Traumatic Stress Disorder (P T S D) is a mental health condition triggered by experiencing or witnessing a traumatic event. It is not limited to soldiers or first responders—anyone who has lived through a deeply distressing event, such as an accident, assault, or natural disaster, can develop P T S D.

Symptoms **of** P T S D

1. **Intrusive Memories**:
   - Flashbacks or vivid recollections of the traumatic event.
   - Nightmares that cause sleep disturbances.
   - Feeling as though the event is happening again (dissociation).
2. **Avoidance**:
   - Steering clear of people, places, or situations that might remind them of the trauma.
   - Suppressing thoughts or feelings related to the event.
3. **Hyperarousal**:

- Constant feeling of being "on edge."
- Difficulty concentrating or relaxing.
- Irritability and heightened startle response.

4. **Negative Changes in Mood**:
   - Persistent guilt, shame, or hopelessness.
   - Loss of interest in activities once enjoyed.
   - Feeling detached or isolated from others.

Real-World Example of P T S D

Sarah, a 34-year-old nurse, survived a car accident. Months later, she finds herself unable to drive, experience panic attacks when hearing screeching tires, and avoid roads altogether. She has nightmares about the accident and feels as if it's her fault, even though she wasn't to blame. Sarah's symptoms illustrate how P T S D can impact daily life, relationships, and mental health.

What Is Anxiety?

Anxiety is the body's natural response to stress, but when it becomes overwhelming or persistent, it shifts from a helpful alert system to a debilitating condition. While everyone feels anxious from time to time, clinical anxiety interferes with daily life and often appears without an obvious cause.

Symptoms of Anxiety

1. **Physical Symptoms**:
   - Racing heartbeat, sweating, or trembling.
   - Shortness of breath or chest tightness.
   - Gastrointestinal issues, like nausea or stomach aches.
2. **Emotional Symptoms**:
   - Persistent feelings of dread or fear.
   - Irrational worries about future events or unlikely scenarios.
3. **Behavioral Symptoms**:

- Avoidance of situations or tasks that trigger anxiety.
- Difficulty relaxing or sitting still.

Types of Anxiety Disorders

- **Generalized Anxiety Disorder (GAD)**: Persistent, excessive worry about various aspects of life (work, family, health).
- **Social Anxiety Disorder**: Intense fear of judgment or embarrassment in social settings.
- **Panic Disorder**: Sudden, repeated panic attacks marked by overwhelming fear and physical symptoms.
- **Specific Phobias**: Fear of a particular object, situation, or activity, such as flying or heights.

Real-World Example of Anxiety

John, a 28-year-old teacher, begins experiencing anxiety before school every morning. His heart races, and he feels dizzy when thinking about standing in front of the class. Though he loves teaching, his fear of making mistakes or being judged is becoming unbearable. John's experience highlights how anxiety can interfere with personal passions and professional life.

What Is Emotional Trauma?

Emotional trauma occurs when an event or series of events overwhelms a person's ability to cope, leaving them with feelings of helplessness, fear, or distress. Unlike P T S D, which often has distinct diagnostic criteria, emotional trauma can be more subtle and long-lasting, stemming from various experiences.

Types of Emotional Trauma

1. **Single-Event Trauma**:

- A one-time event, such as a breakup, accident, or job loss.
2. **Chronic Trauma**:
   - Ongoing stress, such as bullying, domestic violence, or living in an unsafe environment.
3. **Complex Trauma**:
   - Resulting from repeated exposure to harmful situations, often in childhood, such as neglect or abuse.

Symptoms of Emotional Trauma

- Emotional numbness or detachment.
- Difficulty trusting others or forming close relationships.
- Persistent feelings of shame, guilt, or self-blame.
- Emotional flashbacks triggered by unrelated events.

Real-World Example of Emotional Trauma

Emma, a 40-year-old mother, grew up in a household with frequent verbal abuse. Although she now lives a stable life, she finds herself withdrawing from close relationships, fearing conflict or rejection. Emma struggles with self-esteem issues and experiences emotional outbursts when reminded of her past. Her story demonstrates how emotional trauma can linger long after the events themselves.

Key Differences and Overlaps

While P T S D, anxiety, and emotional trauma are distinct, they often coexist:

- Someone with P T S D may develop chronic anxiety as they anticipate future triggers.
- Emotional trauma can lead to anxiety disorders or post-traumatic symptoms if left unaddressed.

- Shared symptoms like avoidance, hyperarousal, and emotional distress blur the lines between these conditions.

By recognizing these conditions and their interconnections, readers can better understand their own experiences or those of loved ones.

Hope for Healing

Understanding these challenges is the first step toward healing. P T S D, anxiety, and emotional trauma are not signs of weakness but natural responses to extraordinary circumstances. They do not have to define a person's life. With therapies like E M D R, individuals can process their pain, regain control, and build resilience for a brighter future.

This book offers practical tools and relatable stories to guide readers on their journey. You are not alone, and healing is possible. Let this knowledge empower you as you take the next steps toward recovery and emotional well-being.

Why It Stands Out: Unique Insights into Trauma and the Wide Applicability of E M D R

E M D R (Eye Movement Desensitization and Reprocessing) therapy is renowned for its effectiveness in treating trauma, but its power extends far beyond the conventional understanding of trauma's effects. What makes this book stand out is its exploration of **lesser-known impacts of trauma** and the emphasis on how E M D R can address these varied and often overlooked aspects of human experience. By uncovering these insights, this chapter expands the reader's understanding of trauma and demonstrates the versatility of E M D R in treating a broad range of challenges.

Lesser-Known Effects of Trauma

When most people think of trauma, they associate it with flashbacks, anxiety, and depression. While these are common symptoms, trauma manifests in many other ways, often going unnoticed or misunderstood. Here are some of the lesser-known effects of trauma that this book addresses:

1. Trauma's Impact on Physical Health

- **Chronic Pain**: Trauma survivors often experience unexplained chronic pain, such as migraines, fibromyalgia, or back pain. These conditions are linked to the body's inability to release the stress stored during traumatic experiences.
- **Immune System Dysfunction**: Trauma disrupts the body's stress-response system, leading to inflammation and increased susceptibility to illnesses.
- **Digestive Disorders**: Conditions like irritable bowel syndrome (IBS) are common among trauma survivors due to the gut-brain connection and prolonged stress.

2. Trauma and Memory

- **Fragmented Memories**: Trauma can cause memories to be stored in fragmented or disorganized ways, making it difficult to recall events clearly. Survivors might remember sensations or emotions but lack a coherent narrative of the experience.
- **Overgeneralized Memories**: Instead of recalling specific events, trauma survivors may develop a tendency to view their past through a lens of negativity, affecting their ability to form positive associations.

3. Social and Relational Effects

- **Hyper-Independence**: Trauma survivors may develop an extreme need for self-reliance, often stemming from a belief that others cannot be trusted or relied upon.
- **Emotional Detachment**: Some individuals become emotionally numb, unable to connect deeply with others, even loved ones.
- **Fear of Intimacy**: Past experiences of betrayal or harm can lead to difficulties in forming close, trusting relationships.

4. Behavioral Changes

- **Risk-Taking Behaviors**: To escape emotional pain, trauma survivors may engage in high-risk behaviors such as substance abuse, reckless driving, or compulsive spending.
- **Perfectionism**: Trauma can manifest as an intense need for control, often expressed through perfectionist tendencies.
- **Over-Attunement to Others**: Survivors may become hyper-aware of others' emotions, often at the expense of their own needs and boundaries.

5. Cognitive and Identity Effects

- **Distorted Self-Perception**: Survivors may internalize guilt or shame, leading to a negative self-image and feelings of unworthiness.
- **Black-and-White Thinking**: Trauma often results in rigid thinking patterns, making it difficult for individuals to see nuances in situations.
- **Loss of Sense of Time**: Many trauma survivors feel "stuck" in the past, unable to fully engage with the present or plan for the future.

Wide Applicability of E M D R

While E M D R is best known for treating P T S D, its applications extend far beyond this single diagnosis. Its versatility makes it a valuable tool for addressing a variety of challenges and conditions.

1. Everyday Stress and Anxiety

E M D R is not limited to life-altering trauma. It can be used to process everyday stressors and anxieties, helping individuals develop healthier coping mechanisms and a greater sense of calm.

2. Grief and Loss

Grief is a complex emotional response that often involves feelings of guilt, anger, and helplessness. E M D R helps individuals reprocess painful memories and find acceptance, allowing them to move forward without feeling "stuck" in their grief.

3. Childhood Trauma and Attachment Issues

E M D R is particularly effective for addressing wounds from childhood, including:

- Neglect or abandonment.
- Emotional or physical abuse.
- Difficulties stemming from insecure attachment styles.

4. Phobias and Fears

E M D R can help individuals overcome specific phobias, such as fear of flying, heights, or public speaking. By reprocessing the underlying memories or associations, it reduces the intensity of the fear response.

5. Addiction and Compulsive Behaviors

Addictions often stem from unresolved trauma or emotional pain. E M D R addresses the root causes, helping individuals break free from destructive patterns.

6. Performance Enhancement

Surprisingly, E M D R is also used to enhance performance in areas such as sports, academics, and public speaking. By targeting the emotional blocks or limiting beliefs that hold people back, E M D R empowers them to reach their full potential.

7. Chronic Illness and Pain Management

Trauma and chronic pain are closely linked. E M D R can help reduce the emotional burden of living with chronic pain, allowing individuals to manage their symptoms more effectively.

8. Cultural and Systemic Trauma

E M D R's adaptability makes it suitable for addressing trauma stemming from systemic issues, such as racism, discrimination, or historical events. This application is especially important for individuals and communities affected by generational trauma.

Why E M D R Works Across Diverse Challenges

The reason E M D R is so versatile lies in its approach. Unlike traditional therapies that focus on talk or behavior modification, E M D R targets the way traumatic memories are stored in the brain. By accessing and reprocessing these memories, E M D R not only alleviates symptoms but also resolves the root causes of distress.

This mechanism makes it effective across a wide spectrum of conditions and experiences, from minor stress to life-altering trauma.

Real-Life Success Stories

To illustrate its wide applicability, this book includes inspiring accounts such as:

- A war veteran overcoming P T S D and reclaiming his sense of purpose.
- A teacher resolving performance anxiety and finding confidence in the classroom.
- A young professional breaking free from the perfectionism rooted in childhood trauma.

These stories highlight E M D R's transformative power and its ability to meet individuals where they are, no matter their challenges.

Chapter 2: The Science Behind E M D R

Eye Movement Desensitization and Reprocessing (E M D R) therapy is not just a buzzword in psychology—it's a groundbreaking approach rooted in scientific research. This chapter dives into the mechanisms that make E M D R effective, unraveling the complexities of how it works and why it is such a powerful tool for healing trauma, anxiety, and emotional wounds.

Understanding the science behind E M D R helps readers appreciate its unique approach and builds confidence in its ability to bring about profound change.

The Foundations of E M D R

Developed by Dr. Francine Shapiro in 1987, E M D R therapy emerged as an innovative solution for addressing trauma. Shapiro discovered that certain types of eye movements could help alleviate the distress associated with traumatic memories. Over the years, this discovery has been refined into an eight-phase therapeutic approach, recognized worldwide as a gold standard for trauma treatment.

At its core, E M D R operates on two key principles:

1. **Adaptive Information Processing (AIP) Model**: The idea that the brain has a natural ability to process and integrate information, but this system can become disrupted by trauma.
2. **Bilateral Stimulation (BLS)**: The use of alternating left-right stimulation (such as eye movements, taps, or tones) to help the brain reprocess traumatic memories.

The Adaptive Information Processing Model

The AIP model serves as the theoretical foundation of E M D R therapy. It posits that:

- The brain is designed to process experiences in a way that promotes learning and emotional resolution.
- Trauma disrupts this process, leaving memories "stuck" in an unprocessed state. These memories remain as raw, emotionally charged fragments, triggering distress whenever they are recalled or triggered.

How Trauma Affects Memory Processing

In a healthy brain, memories are stored and integrated into a larger narrative, allowing individuals to learn from their experiences without being overwhelmed by them. Trauma interrupts this process:

- The **amygdala**, the brain's alarm system, becomes hyperactive, encoding the memory with intense fear and emotional reactivity.
- The **hippocampus**, responsible for placing memories in context, fails to do so, leading to fragmented recollections.
- The **prefrontal cortex**, which governs rational thinking, struggles to regulate the emotional intensity of the memory.

As a result, the traumatic memory remains vivid, raw, and easily triggered, causing distress and symptoms like flashbacks, anxiety, or emotional numbness.

E M D R's Role in Restoring Balance

E M D R helps the brain "unstick" these memories, allowing them to be reprocessed and stored in a way that is no longer emotionally overwhelming. This is achieved through bilateral stimulation, which reactivates the brain's natural processing abilities.

The Science of Bilateral Stimulation

Bilateral stimulation (BLS) is the hallmark of E M D R therapy. It involves rhythmic, alternating stimulation of the left and right sides of the brain through:

- **Eye Movements**: Following the therapist's fingers or a light bar.
- **Tactile Stimulation**: Tapping on the hands or knees.
- **Auditory Stimulation**: Listening to alternating tones through headphones.

How BLS Works

While the exact mechanisms are still being studied, research suggests that BLS:

1. **Engages Both Hemispheres of the Brain**: Trauma is often stored in the right hemisphere, where emotions and sensory memories dominate. BLS activates the left hemisphere, promoting logical processing and integration of the memory.
2. **Mimics REM Sleep**: The eye movements in E M D R are thought to replicate the rapid eye movements of REM sleep, a stage during which the brain naturally processes and consolidates memories.
3. **Reduces Emotional Reactivity**: BLS dampens the intensity of the amygdala's response, allowing individuals to recall traumatic events without being overwhelmed by fear or distress.

Scientific Studies Supporting BLS

Numerous studies have demonstrated the effectiveness of BLS in reducing symptoms of P T S D and anxiety:

- A 2014 meta-analysis found that E M D R significantly reduced P T S D symptoms compared to traditional talk therapy.
- Neuroimaging studies have shown decreased activity in the amygdala and increased connectivity between the hippocampus and prefrontal cortex after E M D R sessions.

The Eight Phases of E M D R Therapy

The structured nature of E M D R therapy ensures that clients are guided through a safe and effective healing process. Here's a brief overview of the eight phases and their scientific underpinnings:

1. **History Taking**: The therapist gathers information about the client's past, identifying target memories and symptoms.
   - **Why It Works**: Provides a clear roadmap for treatment, ensuring the therapy is tailored to the individual's needs.
2. **Preparation**: The therapist helps the client develop coping mechanisms, such as relaxation techniques.
   - **Why It Works**: Prepares the client to handle potential distress during reprocessing.
3. **Assessment**: The target memory is identified, and the client's emotional and physical reactions to it are explored.
   - **Why It Works**: Establishes a baseline for measuring progress.
4. **Desensitization**: BLS is used to help the client reprocess the traumatic memory, reducing its emotional charge.
   - **Why It Works**: Facilitates the integration of the memory into the larger narrative of the client's life.
5. **Installation**: Positive beliefs are reinforced to replace negative ones associated with the memory.

- **Why It Works**: Strengthens resilience and fosters a healthier self-image.
6. **Body Scan**: The client focuses on any lingering physical sensations related to the memory.
   - **Why It Works**: Ensures that trauma is processed not only mentally but also physically.
7. **Closure**: The session ends with techniques to stabilize the client if needed.
   - **Why It Works**: Reinforces a sense of safety and control.
8. **Reevaluation**: Progress is assessed, and any remaining distress is addressed in future sessions.
   - **Why It Works**: Ensures that healing is complete and lasting.

Unique Benefits of E M D R

What sets E M D R apart from traditional therapies is its efficiency and depth:

- **Rapid Results**: Many clients experience significant relief in fewer sessions compared to other forms of therapy.
- **Non-Invasive**: Unlike talk therapy, E M D R doesn't require clients to delve into every detail of their trauma, making it less re-traumatizing.
- **Holistic Approach**: E M D R addresses both the emotional and physical aspects of trauma, offering comprehensive healing.

Real-World Applications

The scientific principles of E M D R make it highly versatile, allowing it to be applied to a wide range of conditions, including:

- P T S D and trauma-related disorders.
- Anxiety, phobias, and panic disorders.
- Addictions and compulsive behaviors.

- Performance anxiety and self-esteem issues.

Case studies in this book illustrate how E M D R has transformed lives, from a firefighter overcoming flashbacks of a rescue gone wrong to a college student breaking free from the anxiety that held her back.

How E M D R Works: A Deep Dive into the Science and Psychology

E M D R (Eye Movement Desensitization and Reprocessing) therapy is a revolutionary approach to healing trauma, anxiety, and emotional wounds. Its effectiveness is rooted in a blend of neuroscience, psychology, and therapeutic practice, making it one of the most researched and validated methods for trauma recovery. This section offers a deep dive into how E M D R works, breaking down its mechanisms and backing its efficacy with cutting-edge scientific and psychological studies.

The Neuroscience Behind E M D R

To understand how E M D R works, it's essential to grasp how the brain processes and stores traumatic memories. In normal circumstances, the brain effectively organizes and integrates experiences into a coherent narrative. However, trauma disrupts this natural process, leaving memories fragmented and emotionally charged.

Trauma and the Brain

1. **Amygdala (The Alarm System)**
   - The amygdala is responsible for detecting threats and triggering the "fight-or-flight" response. During trauma, it becomes hyperactive, encoding the memory with fear and emotional intensity.
   - In P T S D or severe anxiety, the amygdala continues to respond to reminders of the

trauma as if the threat were ongoing, leading to heightened fear and hypervigilance.

2. **Hippocampus (The Memory Organizer)**
   - The hippocampus helps contextualize memories and integrate them into a timeline. Trauma disrupts its function, leaving memories disorganized and "stuck" in a raw, unprocessed state.
   - This is why trauma survivors often feel as though the event is happening in the present, even years later.

3. **Prefrontal Cortex (The Rational Brain)**
   - The prefrontal cortex regulates emotions and helps us make sense of our experiences. Trauma can impair this area, making it difficult to think logically or manage emotional responses.

E M D R's Role in Rewiring the Brain

E M D R helps "unstick" traumatic memories and reprocesses them in a way that reduces their emotional intensity. By combining bilateral stimulation (BLS) with guided recall of the traumatic memory, E M D R activates the brain's natural healing mechanisms.

The Eight Phases of E M D R Therapy

The structured approach of E M D R ensures a safe and effective path to healing. Each phase is designed to guide the client through processing trauma in a manageable and transformative way.

1. **History Taking**
   - The therapist identifies the client's traumatic memories, triggers, and symptoms.
   - Scientific Backing: Research shows that identifying specific traumatic memories is critical for targeted interventions.

2. **Preparation**
    - The therapist equips the client with relaxation techniques and coping strategies to handle potential emotional distress.
    - Scientific Backing: Studies highlight the importance of building a sense of safety and trust before trauma processing begins.
3. **Assessment**
    - The client identifies the target memory and associated negative beliefs, emotions, and body sensations.
    - Scientific Backing: This phase uses principles of cognitive-behavioral therapy (CBT) to pinpoint cognitive distortions tied to trauma.
4. **Desensitization**
    - The client focuses on the memory while engaging in BLS, such as moving their eyes side-to-side.
    - Scientific Backing: Neuroimaging studies reveal that BLS reduces amygdala activity, diminishing the emotional intensity of the memory.
5. **Installation**
    - Positive beliefs (e.g., "I am safe now") are reinforced to replace negative ones (e.g., "I am powerless").
    - Scientific Backing: This phase taps into the brain's neuroplasticity, encouraging the formation of healthier neural pathways.
6. **Body Scan**
    - The client focuses on any lingering physical sensations tied to the memory.
    - Scientific Backing: Trauma is stored in the body as well as the mind. This phase helps release physical tension associated with trauma.
7. **Closure**
    - The therapist ensures the client feels stable and empowered at the end of the session.

- Scientific Backing: This phase promotes emotional regulation and helps consolidate therapeutic gains.

8. **Reevaluation**
   - Progress is reviewed, and unresolved aspects of the memory are addressed in future sessions.
   - Scientific Backing: Studies emphasize the importance of ongoing evaluation to ensure lasting results.

Bilateral Stimulation: The Core Mechanism

Bilateral stimulation (BLS) is the defining feature of E M D R. It involves rhythmic, alternating stimulation of the left and right sides of the body through:

- **Eye Movements**: Following the therapist's hand or a light bar.
- **Tactile Stimulation**: Tapping on alternate hands or knees.
- **Auditory Stimulation**: Listening to tones that alternate between ears.

How BLS Works

- **Engages Both Hemispheres of the Brain**: BLS activates the left (logical) and right (emotional) hemispheres, promoting better communication between them.
- **Mimics REM Sleep**: REM sleep is when the brain naturally processes and consolidates memories. BLS replicates this process while the client is awake and focused on the traumatic memory.
- **Calms the Nervous System**: BLS reduces hyperactivity in the amygdala, helping the client recall traumatic memories without overwhelming fear.

Scientific Evidence for BLS

A 2018 study published in *Frontiers in Psychology* found that BLS significantly reduces the emotional intensity of traumatic memories compared to other forms of therapy. Neuroimaging studies also show increased connectivity between the hippocampus and prefrontal cortex after E M D R, enabling better regulation of emotional responses.

E M D R and the Adaptive Information Processing (AIP) Model

The AIP model underpins E M D R therapy, proposing that the brain has a natural ability to process and heal from distressing events. Trauma disrupts this process, leaving memories frozen in time.

How E M D R Reactivates the AIP System

- **Accesses Traumatic Memories**: E M D R activates the memory network containing the traumatic event.
- **Facilitates Integration**: By reducing emotional reactivity, E M D R allows the memory to be integrated into a broader, less distressing narrative.
- **Promotes Learning**: Clients often gain new insights during E M D R sessions, reframing their experience in a more empowering way.

Psychological Studies Supporting E M D R

1. **Meta-Analyses**
   - Multiple meta-analyses confirm that E M D R is as effective as, or more effective than, traditional trauma-focused therapies, with faster results.
   - One 2014 analysis found that E M D R reduces P T S D symptoms significantly, with fewer sessions required compared to cognitive-behavioral therapy (CBT).

2. **Neuroimaging Research**
   - Studies using fMRI and PET scans show that E M D R reduces activity in the amygdala and increases connectivity in brain regions associated with emotional regulation.
3. **Client Outcomes**
   - Research consistently shows high client satisfaction and long-term symptom relief after E M D R, even for those with complex trauma histories.

Why E M D R Is So Effective

- **Targets the Root Cause**: Unlike therapies that focus solely on symptoms, E M D R addresses the unprocessed traumatic memories that fuel distress.
- **Non-Verbal Processing**: Clients don't need to describe every detail of the trauma, making E M D R less re-traumatizing than traditional talk therapies.
- **Holistic Healing**: By engaging both the mind and body, E M D R offers comprehensive relief from the effects of trauma.

Why E M D R Stands Out: Making Complex Science Clear and Accessible

One of the challenges in discussing therapy techniques like E M D R (Eye Movement Desensitization and Reprocessing) is the complexity of the science behind it. The interplay of neuroscience, psychology, and therapeutic processes can feel overwhelming, especially for those without a background in these fields. What makes this book stand out is its ability to simplify these intricate concepts in a way that is easy to understand. Through clear explanations and, when possible, accompanying visuals, this book ensures that readers of all backgrounds can grasp the science of E M D R and apply it effectively.

Simplifying Complex Concepts

Understanding E M D R requires delving into topics like brain function, trauma processing, and memory storage. This book translates these scientific concepts into plain, relatable language, avoiding unnecessary jargon. The goal is not to dilute the science but to make it approachable and meaningful for readers.

Breaking Down the Science

1. **Trauma and Memory Storage**
   - Complex Concept: Trauma disrupts the brain's natural memory-processing system, leaving memories "stuck" in a raw, unprocessed state.
   - Simplified Explanation: Imagine your brain as a filing cabinet. Most experiences get neatly filed away, but trauma scatters the papers across the floor. E M D R helps pick up and organize those scattered papers, reducing the emotional clutter they create.
2. **Bilateral Stimulation (BLS)**
   - Complex Concept: BLS engages both hemispheres of the brain, mimicking REM sleep and promoting memory integration.
   - Simplified Explanation: Think of BLS as the brain's "reset button," helping it reboot and process memories in a calmer, more balanced way.
3. **The Role of the Amygdala**
   - Complex Concept: The amygdala's heightened activity during trauma leads to the overstorage of emotional intensity in memory.
   - Simplified Explanation: The amygdala is like your brain's smoke alarm—it goes off to warn you of danger. Trauma makes it hyper-sensitive, so it keeps going off, even when there's no real fire. E M D R helps quiet the alarm.

Using Visuals to Enhance Clarity

Visual aids play a crucial role in making scientific concepts more tangible. When possible, this book incorporates simple diagrams, charts, and illustrations to complement the explanations.

Example Visuals

1. **Diagram of the Brain in Trauma**
   - Shows the amygdala, hippocampus, and prefrontal cortex, with arrows indicating how trauma disrupts communication between these regions.
   - **How It Helps**: Offers a clear picture of what happens in the brain during trauma and how E M D R restores balance.
2. **Memory Filing Analogy**
   - An illustration of a messy filing cabinet (trauma) versus an organized one (post-E M D R).
   - **How It Helps**: Visualizes the transformation of chaotic, unprocessed memories into organized, neutral ones.
3. **The E M D R Process**
   - A flowchart outlining the eight phases of E M D R therapy, with icons for each phase (e.g., a target for "Assessment," a light bar for "Desensitization").
   - **How It Helps**: Provides an at-a-glance overview of the therapy process, making it less intimidating for beginners.
4. **Bilateral Stimulation in Action**
   - A simple graphic showing eye movements, tapping, or alternating tones with arrows indicating the left-right pattern.
   - **How It Helps**: Demonstrates how BLS works, even for those unfamiliar with the concept.

Relatable Analogies and Examples

Another way this book simplifies complex science is by using analogies and real-world examples. These relatable comparisons bridge the gap between abstract concepts and everyday understanding.

Examples of Analogies

1. **Neuroplasticity**:
   - Complex Concept: The brain's ability to rewire itself and form new connections.
   - Analogy: "Neuroplasticity is like carving a new path through a forest. The more you use the path, the clearer it becomes. E M D R helps you create healthier mental pathways."
2. **Trauma Triggers**:
   - Complex Concept: External or internal stimuli that activate unresolved trauma.
   - Analogy: "Triggers are like stepping on a landmine—it's an unexpected explosion of emotions tied to buried memories. E M D R helps defuse those landmines."
3. **E M D R's Healing Process**:
   - Complex Concept: The reprocessing of traumatic memories into neutral ones.
   - Analogy: "It's like watching an old, scary movie of your life but realizing you're no longer in danger. E M D R changes the way the 'movie' feels, so it's just a story, not a nightmare."

Empowering All Readers

By simplifying the science, this book empowers readers from all walks of life:

- **Clients**: Gain a deeper understanding of the therapy they're undergoing, reducing fear and increasing trust in the process.

- **Caregivers**: Learn how trauma and E M D R work, enabling them to better support loved ones.
- **Mental Health Professionals**: Access a clear framework for explaining E M D R to clients, enhancing therapeutic rapport.

Scientific Evidence for Simplification

Research in education and psychology supports the use of simplification and visuals to improve understanding:

- A 2019 study in *Frontiers in Psychology* found that using visuals alongside text significantly improves comprehension and retention of complex information.
- Analogies and metaphors have been shown to enhance learning by linking new concepts to familiar ideas, making abstract topics easier to grasp.

Chapter 3: Preparing for Your E M D R Journey

Embarking on your E M D R (Eye Movement Desensitization and Reprocessing) journey can be transformative, but like any healing process, preparation is essential. This chapter is designed to guide you through the steps to get ready for E M D R therapy, helping you build a solid foundation for a successful and empowering experience. Whether you're a first-time client or have tried other forms of therapy before, this preparation phase will set you up for meaningful progress.

Why Preparation Is Important

Healing through E M D R is a profound journey that requires emotional, mental, and physical readiness. By preparing in advance, you can:

- Minimize distress during therapy.
- Enhance your ability to stay present and engaged.
- Build resilience to handle difficult emotions that may surface.
- Empower yourself with tools to maintain stability between sessions.

Step 1: Understanding What to Expect

The first step in preparing for E M D R is understanding what the process entails. This knowledge helps reduce anxiety about the unknown and allows you to approach therapy with confidence.

What E M D R Involves

1. **Recall of Traumatic Memories**: You'll be guided to focus on distressing memories while engaging in bilateral stimulation (e.g., eye movements or tapping).

2. **Emotional Processing**: You may experience strong emotions during sessions, but these are temporary and part of the healing process.
3. **Reframing Beliefs**: Negative beliefs tied to the memory (e.g., "I am powerless") will be replaced with healthier, more empowering ones (e.g., "I am strong").
4. **Gradual Progress**: E M D R unfolds in phases, and healing occurs incrementally. Some memories may take multiple sessions to fully process.

Real-Life Example

Karen, a 35-year-old teacher, felt apprehensive before starting E M D R. She imagined reliving her trauma in excruciating detail. However, her therapist explained that E M D R doesn't require her to verbalize every aspect of the memory. This reassurance eased her fears, allowing her to fully commit to the process.

Step 2: Building a Strong Therapeutic Alliance

A good relationship with your therapist is the cornerstone of successful E M D R therapy. It's crucial to find someone you feel comfortable with, as trust and communication will play a significant role in your journey.

How to Choose the Right Therapist

1. **Credentials**: Look for a therapist trained and certified in E M D R.
2. **Experience**: Ask about their experience with clients who have similar concerns.
3. **Connection**: During the initial consultation, assess whether you feel heard, respected, and understood.

What to Discuss Before Starting

- Your therapy goals: What do you hope to achieve with E M D R?

- Your trauma history: Share as much as you're comfortable with to help your therapist tailor the approach.
- Your concerns: Voice any fears or misconceptions about E M D R.

Step 3: Developing Emotional Coping Tools

E M D R can bring up strong emotions, so having strategies to manage distress is vital. These tools will help you stay grounded during sessions and maintain stability between them.

Grounding Techniques

1. **Breathing Exercises**:
   - Practice deep belly breathing to calm your nervous system.
   - Example: Inhale for a count of four, hold for four, and exhale for six.
2. **Mindfulness Practices**:
   - Focus on your senses to anchor yourself in the present moment.
   - Example: Name five things you see, four things you feel, three things you hear, two things you smell, and one thing you taste.
3. **Progressive Muscle Relaxation**:
   - Tense and release different muscle groups to reduce physical tension.

Creating a Safe Place

Your therapist may guide you in visualizing a "safe place" during preparation. This mental image serves as a calming retreat you can return to if the session becomes overwhelming.

- **Example**: Imagine a serene beach where you feel peaceful and secure. Focus on the sights, sounds, and sensations to make it vivid.

Step 4: Setting Realistic Expectations

While E M D R is highly effective, it's important to approach it with realistic expectations. Healing is not an overnight process, and progress may vary depending on the complexity of your trauma.

What to Keep in Mind

1. **Healing Is Nonlinear**: You may feel worse before you feel better as old wounds are brought to the surface.
2. **Memories May Resurface**: Previously forgotten memories might come up during therapy. This is a normal part of the healing process.
3. **Patience Is Key**: Allow yourself the time and space needed to fully process your experiences.

Step 5: Preparing Your Environment

Your surroundings play a significant role in supporting your E M D R journey. Creating a calm, supportive environment can help you stay focused and reduce stress.

Before the Session

- **Schedule Downtime**: Avoid packing your day with activities immediately before or after a session.
- **Choose Comfortable Clothing**: Wear something that helps you feel at ease.

After the Session

- **Practice Self-Care**: Engage in soothing activities, such as taking a warm bath, journaling, or spending time in nature.
- **Stay Connected**: Reach out to supportive friends or family members if you feel emotionally vulnerable.

Step 6: Journaling and Reflection

Keeping a journal can enhance your E M D R experience by helping you track progress, identify triggers, and process emotions between sessions.

What to Journal

- Memories or emotions that surface during or after sessions.
- Insights or realizations about your trauma and beliefs.
- Any improvements in symptoms or emotional resilience.

Example Entry

"Today, I felt a strong wave of sadness during my session. It reminded me of feeling abandoned as a child. My therapist helped me reframe it, and now I'm beginning to see that I deserved love and care, even if I didn't always receive it."

Step 7: Engaging Your Support System

Healing is not something you have to do alone. A strong support system can provide encouragement, perspective, and emotional safety as you navigate your E M D R journey.

How to Involve Others

- Share your goals and progress with trusted loved ones.

- Ask for practical support, such as helping with daily tasks if you feel drained after sessions.
- Join a support group to connect with others who understand your experience.

What Readers Will Learn: Step-by-Step Guidance on Preparing Mentally and Emotionally for E M D R Therapy

E M D R therapy (Eye Movement Desensitization and Reprocessing) offers a transformative approach to healing trauma, anxiety, and emotional wounds. However, its effectiveness can be significantly enhanced when clients take time to prepare both mentally and emotionally for the process. This section provides a comprehensive, step-by-step guide to help readers approach E M D R therapy with the tools and mindset necessary for a successful and empowering journey.

Step 1: Understand the Basics of E M D R

Before beginning E M D R therapy, it's essential to have a clear understanding of what it entails. Familiarity with the process can reduce apprehension and help you approach the therapy with confidence.

Learn the Eight Phases of E M D R

- **History Taking**: Sharing your background and identifying target memories.
- **Preparation**: Developing skills to manage distress.
- **Assessment**: Evaluating your emotional and physical responses to target memories.
- **Desensitization**: Reprocessing the memory with bilateral stimulation.
- **Installation**: Reinforcing positive beliefs to replace negative ones.
- **Body Scan**: Addressing residual physical sensations.
- **Closure**: Stabilizing at the end of each session.

- **Reevaluation**: Reviewing progress and planning next steps.

Know What to Expect

- You'll focus on distressing memories while engaging in bilateral stimulation, such as eye movements or tapping.
- Emotional intensity may rise during sessions but will decrease over time as the memory is reprocessed.

Step 2: Address Fears and Misconceptions

Many people approach E M D R with uncertainty or fear about revisiting painful memories. Addressing these concerns beforehand can help you feel more secure.

Common Concerns

- **Fear of Reliving Trauma**: While E M D R involves recalling traumatic memories, you are not reliving them in real time. The goal is to reprocess these memories in a safe and controlled way.
- **Worry About Emotional Overwhelm**: Your therapist will provide tools to help you manage any distress that arises during sessions.

How to Address Them

- **Educate Yourself**: Read about E M D R, its success rates, and its safety.
- **Speak with Your Therapist**: Share your concerns during the initial consultation. A good therapist will address these openly and provide reassurance.

Step 3: Establish Goals for Therapy

Having clear goals can give your therapy a sense of purpose and direction, making it easier to measure progress.

Examples of Goals

- Reducing the emotional intensity of a specific memory.
- Overcoming avoidance behaviors tied to trauma triggers.
- Building self-confidence and replacing negative beliefs with positive ones.

How to Set Goals

1. Write down the areas of your life most affected by trauma or anxiety.
2. Discuss these with your therapist to identify priorities.
3. Create specific, achievable objectives (e.g., "I want to feel less anxious in crowded spaces").

Step 4: Develop Emotional Coping Skills

E M D R often brings up strong emotions, so it's crucial to have strategies in place to manage distress during and between sessions.

Techniques to Practice

1. **Deep Breathing**: Slow, controlled breaths can help regulate your nervous system. For example, inhale for four counts, hold for four, and exhale for six.
2. **Grounding Exercises**: Anchor yourself in the present moment by focusing on sensory details, such as the feel of your feet on the ground or the sound of your breathing.
3. **Mindfulness Meditation**: Practice observing your thoughts and emotions without judgment. Apps like Headspace or Calm can be helpful for beginners.
4. **Progressive Muscle Relaxation**: Tense and release each muscle group in your body to release physical tension.

Build a Safe Place Visualization

Your therapist may guide you in creating a mental "safe place" to retreat to if therapy becomes overwhelming. This can be a peaceful beach, a cozy room, or any setting where you feel secure.

Step 5: Strengthen Your Support System

Healing is not a solitary journey. Surrounding yourself with supportive individuals can provide comfort and encouragement.

Who Can Help

- Trusted friends or family members who understand and respect your healing process.
- Support groups for individuals with similar experiences.
- A therapist or counselor outside of E M D R sessions for additional emotional support.

How to Involve Them

- Share your goals and progress with those you trust.
- Let them know how they can help, whether it's simply listening or offering practical support, like childcare or transportation to sessions.

Step 6: Cultivate a Growth Mindset

Your mindset plays a significant role in your readiness for E M D R therapy. Approaching therapy with an attitude of openness and resilience can make a difference in your experience.

Shift Your Perspective

- Instead of viewing therapy as revisiting pain, see it as an opportunity for healing and growth.
- Recognize that healing is a process, not an instant fix. Be patient with yourself.

Affirmations to Practice

- "I am taking steps to reclaim my life."
- "It's okay to feel uncomfortable—healing comes from facing challenges."
- "I am stronger than my trauma."

Step 7: Prepare Your Environment

Creating a calming and supportive environment can enhance your mental and emotional readiness for E M D R.

Before Sessions

- **Plan for Downtime**: Avoid scheduling stressful activities immediately before or after therapy.
- **Wear Comfortable Clothing**: Choose attire that helps you feel relaxed and at ease.

After Sessions

- **Practice Self-Care**: Engage in activities that soothe and replenish you, such as taking a warm bath, journaling, or spending time in nature.
- **Give Yourself Time**: Allow space to reflect and process any emotions that arise.

Step 8: Keep a Journal

Journaling can be a valuable tool for tracking progress, identifying triggers, and processing emotions.

What to Write

- **Pre-Session**: Note your feelings, thoughts, and expectations before therapy.
- **Post-Session**: Reflect on what came up during the session and any insights or emotions you experienced.
- **Between Sessions**: Document any changes in your symptoms, as well as successes or challenges in daily life.

Step 9: Practice Self-Compassion

Healing is not linear, and setbacks are part of the process. Treat yourself with kindness and patience as you navigate your E M D R journey.

How to Foster Self-Compassion

- **Acknowledge Your Strength**: Recognize the courage it takes to face your trauma and seek healing.
- **Celebrate Small Wins**: Every step forward, no matter how small, is a victory.
- **Be Gentle with Yourself**: If emotions feel overwhelming, remind yourself that it's part of the healing process and that you're doing your best.

Why It Stands Out: Self-Assessment Tools, Checklists, and Exercises to Gauge Readiness for E M D R

What sets this book apart is its inclusion of practical self-assessment tools, checklists, and exercises that empower readers to evaluate their readiness for E M D R therapy. Preparing for therapy can feel overwhelming, especially when facing the prospect of addressing deeply rooted trauma. These resources provide a structured and supportive approach to help readers assess where they are emotionally, mentally, and practically before embarking on their E M D R journey.

1. Self-Assessment Tools

The self-assessment tools in this book are designed to help readers reflect on their trauma history, emotional state, and current coping mechanisms. These tools are user-friendly and accessible, allowing readers to identify their strengths and areas for improvement.

A. Trauma Impact Assessment

This tool helps readers identify the ways trauma has affected their lives, guiding them to understand the areas that may need healing.

Questions to Reflect On:

1. How often do you experience intrusive thoughts or memories about a past event?
2. Do you avoid specific people, places, or activities because they remind you of a traumatic experience?
3. Do you feel emotionally numb or disconnected from others?
4. How often do you feel on edge, easily startled, or hypervigilant?
5. Have you noticed any physical symptoms (e.g., headaches, stomach issues) that might be related to stress or trauma?

Scoring:

- 1-3: Minimal trauma impact; may benefit from E M D R for specific issues.
- 4-7: Moderate trauma impact; E M D R could help address unresolved distress.
- 8+: Severe trauma impact; prioritizing E M D R therapy could lead to significant relief.

B. Emotional Readiness Scale

This tool evaluates emotional stability and readiness to engage with potentially distressing memories during therapy.

Rate Yourself on a Scale of 1 (Strongly Disagree) to 5 (Strongly Agree):

1. I feel comfortable experiencing strong emotions, even if they are uncomfortable.
2. I have strategies in place to calm myself when I feel overwhelmed.
3. I trust my ability to navigate difficult situations with support.
4. I am open to exploring painful memories in a safe environment.
5. I am committed to my healing journey, even if it feels challenging.

Interpretation:

- Scores of 15+: Ready to begin E M D R therapy.
- Scores below 15: Consider working with a therapist on emotional regulation skills before starting E M D R.

2. Checklists

Checklists offer a practical way for readers to track their progress and ensure they've addressed key aspects of preparation. These structured lists make the journey to E M D R therapy feel manageable and organized.

A. Pre-Therapy Preparation Checklist

Before starting E M D R, it's important to set the stage for success. Use this checklist to confirm your readiness:

✓ I have researched and understand the basics of E M D R therapy.

✓ I have identified a certified E M D R therapist I trust.

✓ I have set clear therapy goals with my therapist.

✓ I have learned at least two grounding techniques to manage emotional distress.

✓ I have created a "safe place" visualization to use during therapy.

✓ I have a support system in place for emotional support outside of therapy.

✓ I have set aside time in my schedule to focus on my therapy journey.

B. Post-Session Care Checklist

After an E M D R session, self-care is essential to process emotions and maintain stability. Use this checklist to ensure you're taking care of yourself:

✓ I have scheduled downtime after my session to rest and reflect.

✓ I have a journal ready to document my thoughts and feelings.

✓ I have engaged in a calming activity, such as taking a walk, meditating, or spending time with a loved one.

✓ I have avoided making major decisions immediately after the session.

✓ I have reached out to my support network if I felt emotionally vulnerable.

3. Exercises to Enhance Readiness

Exercises included in this book are designed to build resilience and prepare readers for the emotional work of E M D R therapy. These practical activities can be completed at home and help readers develop the skills they'll need during therapy.

A. Building a Safe Place Visualization

This exercise helps readers create a mental "safe place" to use during E M D R sessions if emotions become overwhelming.

Steps:

1. Close your eyes and imagine a place where you feel completely safe and at peace. This could be a real location or a made-up space.
2. Focus on the sensory details:
   - What do you see? (e.g., a sunny beach, a cozy cabin)
   - What do you hear? (e.g., ocean waves, birds singing)
   - What do you feel? (e.g., warm sun on your skin, a soft blanket)
3. Practice returning to this visualization daily to strengthen its calming effect.

B. Identifying Triggers

This exercise helps readers pinpoint situations, emotions, or memories that may come up during E M D R sessions.

Steps:

1. Write down situations or interactions that make you feel anxious, angry, or sad.
2. Reflect on why these moments might be triggering— are they tied to past events or beliefs?
3. Share your findings with your therapist to inform your E M D R process.

C. Practicing Emotional Regulation

This exercise builds the emotional resilience needed to face difficult memories.

Steps:

1. Identify a mildly distressing memory or thought.
2. Focus on it for a few seconds, noticing any emotional or physical reactions.
3. Use a grounding technique, such as deep breathing or progressive muscle relaxation, to calm yourself.
4. Reflect on how the technique helped and repeat as needed.

How These Tools Empower Readers

- **Clarity**: Self-assessment tools help readers understand where they are on their healing journey.
- **Confidence**: Checklists ensure that no critical step is overlooked, giving readers peace of mind.
- **Skill-Building**: Exercises prepare readers for the emotional demands of E M D R therapy, helping them approach it with resilience and focus.
- **Personalization**: Each tool allows readers to tailor their preparation to their unique needs and experiences.

Chapter 4: The E M D R Process: A Step-by-Step Guide

Eye Movement Desensitization and Reprocessing (E M D R) therapy is a structured and comprehensive approach to addressing trauma, anxiety, and emotional wounds. The process unfolds across eight clearly defined phases, each designed to guide the individual safely and effectively toward healing. In this chapter, we break down the E M D R process step by step, providing readers with a clear understanding of what to expect at each stage.

Overview of the Eight Phases

E M D R therapy is built around the **Adaptive Information Processing (AIP) model**, which posits that the brain has a natural ability to process and heal from distressing experiences. Trauma disrupts this system, and E M D R helps restart it. Each phase of E M D R is carefully designed to facilitate healing while ensuring the safety and stability of the individual.

Phase 1: History Taking

The first phase is about creating a comprehensive picture of the client's past, present, and future challenges.

What Happens in This Phase?

- The therapist collects information about the client's trauma history and current symptoms.
- Together, they identify specific target memories to address during therapy, along with any triggers or patterns of distress.
- The therapist assesses the client's readiness for E M D R and establishes goals for therapy.

Why It's Important

This phase ensures that the therapy is tailored to the client's unique needs. It also lays the groundwork for a focused and effective healing process.

Phase 2: Preparation

In this phase, the therapist helps the client develop the tools and skills necessary to handle the emotional intensity of reprocessing memories.

What Happens in This Phase?

- The therapist explains the E M D R process, addressing any questions or concerns.
- The client practices grounding techniques, such as deep breathing, progressive muscle relaxation, or visualization.
- A "safe place" is established—a calming mental image that the client can return to during sessions if they feel overwhelmed.

Why It's Important

Preparation builds trust between the client and therapist and equips the client with the emotional tools needed to navigate the upcoming phases safely.

Phase 3: Assessment

The therapist and client narrow their focus to a specific traumatic memory, breaking it down into its emotional, physical, and cognitive components.

What Happens in This Phase?

1. **Identifying the Target Memory**: The client selects a distressing memory to work on.

2. **Negative Beliefs**: The therapist asks the client to identify a negative belief associated with the memory (e.g., "I am powerless" or "I am unlovable").
3. **Positive Beliefs**: A desired positive belief is identified (e.g., "I am in control" or "I am worthy of love").
4. **Emotional and Physical Responses**: The client rates the intensity of their emotional distress and notes any physical sensations linked to the memory.

Why It's Important

This phase helps the therapist and client understand the full scope of the memory's impact, setting a clear target for reprocessing.

Phase 4: Desensitization

The desensitization phase is the heart of E M D R therapy, where the reprocessing of traumatic memories occurs.

What Happens in This Phase?

- The client focuses on the target memory while engaging in **bilateral stimulation** (BLS), such as:
    - Moving their eyes side-to-side.
    - Listening to alternating tones through headphones.
    - Tapping alternately on their knees or hands.
- The therapist periodically asks the client to share what they are experiencing, such as new thoughts, feelings, or sensations.
- The process continues until the memory's emotional charge significantly decreases.

Why It's Important

This phase helps the brain reprocess the memory, reducing its emotional intensity and integrating it into a healthier narrative.

Phase 5: Installation

During the installation phase, the focus shifts to reinforcing positive beliefs that replace the negative ones associated with the memory.

What Happens in This Phase?

- The therapist guides the client in pairing the memory with the previously identified positive belief.
- Using BLS, the positive belief is strengthened, helping the client internalize a healthier perspective (e.g., shifting from "I am powerless" to "I am in control").

Why It's Important

This phase builds resilience and reinforces the client's sense of empowerment, promoting long-term healing.

Phase 6: Body Scan

Trauma often leaves a physical imprint, manifesting as tension, pain, or discomfort in the body. The body scan phase ensures that these physical symptoms are addressed.

What Happens in This Phase?

- The client focuses on their body while thinking about the target memory and the positive belief.
- The therapist helps the client identify any lingering physical sensations related to the memory.
- If tension or discomfort remains, additional BLS may be used to release it.

Why It's Important

This phase ensures that healing is holistic, addressing both the emotional and physical impacts of trauma.

Phase 7: Closure

Each E M D R session ends with a closure phase, designed to stabilize the client and ensure they leave the session feeling grounded.

What Happens in This Phase?

- The therapist guides the client through relaxation or grounding exercises.
- The client reflects on their progress and emotional state.
- The therapist provides strategies for managing any emotions or thoughts that arise between sessions.

Why It's Important

Closure ensures that the client feels safe and supported, even after intense emotional processing.

Phase 8: Reevaluation

Reevaluation occurs at the beginning of each new session, allowing the therapist and client to assess progress and determine next steps.

What Happens in This Phase?

- The therapist checks on the client's emotional state and any changes since the last session.
- Progress on the previously targeted memory is reviewed.
- New targets are identified if needed, and the process begins again.

Why It's Important

This phase ensures that therapy is dynamic and responsive to the client's evolving needs, building on past successes to address unresolved issues.

Why E M D R Works

E M D R's structured approach allows the brain to reprocess traumatic memories in a safe and controlled way, transforming distressing experiences into neutral or even empowering ones. The integration of bilateral stimulation accelerates this process, mimicking the natural healing mechanisms of REM sleep.

Example Journey: Sarah's E M D R Experience

Sarah, a 32-year-old nurse, came to E M D R therapy struggling with flashbacks from a car accident. Over the course of several sessions:

1. She identified the accident as a target memory (Assessment).
2. She practiced deep breathing and visualization to prepare (Preparation).
3. She reprocessed the memory using eye movements, gradually reducing her emotional distress (Desensitization).
4. She replaced her belief of "I am unsafe" with "I am capable of handling challenges" (Installation).
5. She noticed tension in her shoulders and released it through additional BLS (Body Scan).

By the end of her E M D R journey, Sarah no longer experienced flashbacks and felt a renewed sense of control and confidence in her life.

What Readers Will Learn: A Detailed Breakdown of the Eight Phases of E M D R Therapy

E M D R (Eye Movement Desensitization and Reprocessing) therapy is a structured and highly effective method for addressing trauma, anxiety, and emotional distress. Its foundation lies in a systematic approach that unfolds in **eight distinct phases**, each serving a critical role in guiding the client toward healing and recovery. This detailed breakdown helps readers understand how each phase works, what to expect, and why it's essential to the overall process.

Phase 1: History Taking

The first phase focuses on gathering information about the client's past experiences and current challenges. This foundational phase creates a roadmap for the therapy journey.

What Happens in This Phase?

- The therapist conducts a comprehensive assessment of the client's trauma history, symptoms, and triggers.
- Key memories and events that contribute to emotional distress are identified.
- The client's coping mechanisms, strengths, and support systems are evaluated.

Why It's Important

This phase ensures the therapy is personalized to the client's unique needs. By identifying specific targets (e.g., traumatic memories, negative beliefs), the therapist lays the groundwork for effective reprocessing.

Phase 2: Preparation

This phase prepares the client for the emotional work of E M D R. It emphasizes building trust, developing coping skills, and ensuring the client feels safe and supported.

What Happens in This Phase?

- The therapist explains the E M D R process, addressing any questions or concerns.
- Clients are taught grounding techniques, such as deep breathing or visualization, to manage distress during sessions.
- A "safe place" visualization is created—this is a mental image or memory that the client can use as a calming retreat if therapy becomes overwhelming.

Why It's Important

Preparation reduces fear and anxiety about therapy. It equips the client with tools to navigate intense emotions and ensures they feel in control throughout the process.

Phase 3: Assessment

The assessment phase focuses on pinpointing the specific elements of a traumatic memory that will be targeted during therapy.

What Happens in This Phase?

1. **Identify the Target Memory**: The therapist helps the client select a specific memory or event to work on.
2. **Negative Cognition**: The client identifies a negative belief tied to the memory (e.g., "I am powerless" or "I am unlovable").
3. **Positive Cognition**: The client chooses a desired belief they want to replace the negative one (e.g., "I am in control" or "I am worthy of love").

4. **Rate the Emotional Intensity**: The client rates their distress using the **Subjective Units of Disturbance Scale (SUDS)**, where 0 = no distress and 10 = maximum distress.
5. **Physical Sensations**: The client identifies any body sensations linked to the memory (e.g., tightness in the chest, a lump in the throat).

Why It's Important

This phase provides a clear and measurable focus for therapy. It ensures that the memory's emotional, cognitive, and physical components are addressed, leading to more comprehensive healing.

Phase 4: Desensitization

The desensitization phase is where the actual reprocessing of the traumatic memory takes place. This is the core of E M D R therapy.

What Happens in This Phase?

- The client focuses on the target memory while simultaneously engaging in **bilateral stimulation (BLS)**, such as:
    - Following the therapist's finger with their eyes.
    - Listening to alternating tones through headphones.
    - Feeling taps on their hands or knees.
- As the client processes the memory, new thoughts, emotions, and sensations may arise. The therapist helps the client notice and work through these as they emerge.
- The process continues until the memory's emotional charge significantly decreases, as reflected in a lower SUDS score.

Why It's Important

Desensitization helps the brain "unstick" the memory, allowing it to be processed and integrated into a broader narrative. This reduces its emotional intensity and impact.

Phase 5: Installation

Once the memory has been desensitized, the focus shifts to reinforcing positive beliefs that replace the negative ones associated with the memory.

What Happens in This Phase?

- The therapist guides the client to pair the target memory with their positive belief (e.g., replacing "I am powerless" with "I am strong").
- Using BLS, the therapist helps the client strengthen this positive belief, making it more resilient and deeply ingrained.

Why It's Important

Installation promotes a sense of empowerment and self-worth. It helps the client develop healthier perspectives and beliefs that support long-term emotional resilience.

Phase 6: Body Scan

Trauma often manifests in the body as physical tension or discomfort. The body scan phase addresses these lingering physical symptoms to ensure holistic healing.

What Happens in This Phase?

- The client focuses on their body while thinking about the target memory and the positive belief.
- They note any residual physical sensations, such as tightness, aches, or tingling.

- The therapist uses BLS to help release these sensations, promoting a sense of physical relaxation and comfort.

Why It's Important

This phase ensures that healing extends beyond the mind to the body, addressing the physical toll of trauma and fostering a sense of overall well-being.

Phase 7: Closure

Closure is essential for ensuring the client feels stable and supported at the end of each session, especially if the target memory hasn't been fully processed.

What Happens in This Phase?

- The therapist guides the client through relaxation or grounding exercises to calm their nervous system.
- The client reflects on the session, discussing any insights or emotions that arose.
- The therapist provides strategies for managing emotions and thoughts between sessions.

Why It's Important

Closure helps the client leave the session feeling secure and in control, preventing emotional overwhelm. It also reinforces the progress made during the session.

Phase 8: Reevaluation

The final phase focuses on reviewing the client's progress and planning the next steps in therapy.

What Happens in This Phase?

- At the beginning of the next session, the therapist checks in with the client to evaluate their current emotional state.
- The client reflects on any changes they've noticed since the previous session, including improvements in symptoms or triggers.
- If the target memory has been fully processed, the therapist and client identify a new memory or issue to address.

Why It's Important

Reevaluation ensures that therapy is dynamic and responsive to the client's needs. It provides a clear measure of progress and helps maintain momentum toward healing.

Why the Eight Phases Work Together

The structured nature of E M D R therapy ensures a balance between safety, exploration, and healing. Each phase builds on the previous one, creating a seamless flow that allows the client to process trauma in a manageable and transformative way.

Key Takeaways

- **Holistic Healing**: E M D R addresses trauma at emotional, cognitive, and physical levels.
- **Client-Centered**: The process is tailored to each individual's unique experiences and goals.
- **Empowerment**: By replacing negative beliefs with positive ones, E M D R fosters a renewed sense of control and self-worth.
- **Safety First**: The structured phases ensure that the client feels supported and grounded throughout the therapy journey.

Why It Stands Out: Real-World Case Studies Illustrate E M D R in Action

One of the most compelling aspects of this book is its inclusion of real-world case studies, which offer readers a firsthand look at how E M D R (Eye Movement Desensitization and Reprocessing) therapy unfolds in practice. These stories bring the abstract concepts of E M D R to life, making it relatable and easier to understand. By showcasing diverse scenarios, these case studies demonstrate the versatility of E M D R in addressing a wide range of emotional challenges, from trauma and anxiety to phobias and grief.

The Power of Case Studies

Case studies help bridge the gap between theory and practice. They provide readers with:

- **Real-Life Context**: How E M D R is applied to unique situations.
- **Insight into the Process**: A clear understanding of the eight phases in action.
- **Emotional Resonance**: Stories that readers can connect with, offering hope and encouragement.
- **Validation of Effectiveness**: Proof of how E M D R has changed lives for the better.

Featured Case Studies

The following case studies represent different challenges and demonstrate the versatility of E M D R therapy. Each story highlights how the eight phases of E M D R therapy come together to create a transformative experience.

Case Study 1: Overcoming Childhood Trauma

Client Profile: Maria, a 29-year-old social worker, sought E M D R therapy to address flashbacks and nightmares stemming from childhood abuse. She struggled with trust issues and feelings of unworthiness.

How E M D R Unfolded:

1. **History Taking**: Maria shared her background, revealing a pattern of emotional and physical abuse during her childhood. The therapist identified her primary triggers: loud voices and unexpected physical touch.
2. **Preparation**: Maria learned grounding techniques, such as deep breathing and visualization, to manage potential distress during sessions. She created a "safe place" visualization—a meadow with soft sunlight and a gentle breeze.
3. **Assessment**: The therapist and Maria targeted a memory of an incident where she was yelled at and felt powerless. Maria identified the negative belief, "I am worthless," and chose the positive belief, "I am valuable and strong."
4. **Desensitization**: During BLS (eye movements), Maria initially felt intense fear and sadness. As the session progressed, her emotional response diminished, and she began recalling moments of kindness from her childhood that she had previously overlooked.
5. **Installation**: The therapist reinforced Maria's positive belief, helping her internalize "I am valuable and strong."
6. **Body Scan**: Maria noticed tension in her shoulders, which released after additional BLS.
7. **Closure**: Maria ended the session feeling calm and optimistic. She practiced her grounding techniques at home.
8. **Reevaluation**: At her next session, Maria reported fewer flashbacks and an increased ability to trust her partner.

Outcome: Over 12 sessions, Maria developed a sense of self-worth and began forming healthier relationships.

Case Study 2: Healing from a Car Accident

Client Profile: James, a 36-year-old teacher, experienced panic attacks while driving after a near-fatal car accident. He avoided highways and long drives, significantly impacting his life.

How E M D R Unfolded:

1. **History Taking**: James shared the details of the accident and identified his triggers, such as the sound of screeching tires and the sight of headlights approaching.
2. **Preparation**: James practiced progressive muscle relaxation and learned to visualize a peaceful lakeside cabin as his "safe place."
3. **Assessment**: The target memory was the moment of impact during the accident. James identified the negative belief, "I am in danger," and selected the positive belief, "I am safe and capable."
4. **Desensitization**: Through BLS, James began reprocessing the memory. Initially, he relived the fear, but as the session continued, the memory lost its emotional intensity. He began to see the event as something in the past, not a present threat.
5. **Installation**: The positive belief, "I am safe and capable," was strengthened using BLS.
6. **Body Scan**: James noticed a lingering tightness in his chest, which subsided after additional reprocessing.
7. **Closure**: James left the session with a sense of relief and hope. His therapist encouraged him to practice driving short distances while using relaxation techniques.

8. **Reevaluation**: By the next session, James reported driving without panic on local roads and was ready to try highways.

Outcome: Within six sessions, James regained his confidence behind the wheel and began enjoying road trips again.

Case Study 3: Addressing Social Anxiety

Client Profile: Priya, a 24-year-old graduate student, struggled with intense social anxiety, particularly in group settings. She avoided presentations and social events, fearing judgment and embarrassment.

How E M D R Unfolded:

1. **History Taking**: Priya shared her history of being bullied in high school, which contributed to her anxiety. The therapist identified key memories, including a humiliating moment in a school assembly.
2. **Preparation**: Priya practiced mindfulness and self-soothing techniques, such as holding a comforting object, to manage anxiety.
3. **Assessment**: The target memory was the school assembly incident. Priya's negative belief was, "I am inadequate," and her positive belief was, "I am confident and capable."
4. **Desensitization**: During BLS, Priya initially felt overwhelming embarrassment. Gradually, the memory became less vivid, and she began recalling instances where her peers admired her intelligence.
5. **Installation**: The positive belief, "I am confident and capable," was installed, boosting Priya's self-esteem.
6. **Body Scan**: Priya noticed a knot in her stomach, which dissipated after additional BLS.
7. **Closure**: The therapist guided Priya through a relaxation exercise. She left feeling more optimistic about participating in group activities.

8. **Reevaluation**: By the next session, Priya shared that she had successfully spoken up in a seminar without feeling overwhelmed.

Outcome: Over eight sessions, Priya developed greater confidence and began actively participating in social and academic settings.

Why Real-World Case Studies Enhance the Reader's Experience

1. **Provides Tangible Examples**: Readers can see how the abstract concepts of E M D R apply to real-life situations.
2. **Demonstrates Versatility**: The diversity of scenarios—from childhood trauma to specific phobias—highlights E M D R's adaptability.
3. **Offers Hope**: Success stories inspire readers to believe in their own potential for healing.
4. **Clarifies the Process**: By walking through the eight phases step-by-step, case studies demystify the therapy and make it more approachable.

Chapter 5: E M D R for Self-Help: Techniques You Can Practice

Eye Movement Desensitization and Reprocessing (E M D R) is traditionally facilitated by a trained therapist, but aspects of its principles can be adapted into self-help techniques. These methods provide individuals with tools to manage emotional distress, reduce anxiety, and process minor challenges independently. While self-help E M D R cannot replace professional therapy for deep or complex trauma, it can complement therapy and empower you to take charge of your emotional well-being.

This chapter explores E M D R-inspired self-help techniques, offering step-by-step guidance for integrating them into your daily life.

Understanding the Limits of Self-Help E M D R

Before diving into the techniques, it's important to recognize the boundaries of self-help in E M D R:

- **When Self-Help Works**: Managing everyday stress, mild anxiety, or situational triggers. It's also helpful for reinforcing progress made in therapy.
- **When to Seek Professional Help**: If you experience severe trauma, dissociation, overwhelming emotions, or complex P T S D, working with a certified E M D R therapist is essential.

1. Grounding with Bilateral Stimulation (BLS)

Bilateral stimulation (BLS) is a core component of E M D R therapy. It helps activate both hemispheres of the brain, promoting emotional regulation and reducing the intensity of distressing memories or feelings. You can use this technique to calm yourself during moments of stress.

Steps for Self-Guided BLS

1. **Choose a Method**:
   - Tap alternately on your knees or shoulders.
   - Use a pair of headphones to listen to sounds that alternate between your left and right ears.
   - Follow an object moving side-to-side with your eyes (e.g., a pen or your finger).
2. **Focus on a Mildly Distressing Memory or Emotion**:
   - Think of something that's bothering you but isn't overwhelming.
   - Rate your distress on a scale from 0 (no distress) to 10 (maximum distress).
3. **Engage in BLS**:
   - Begin your chosen BLS method for 20–30 seconds while focusing on the memory or feeling.
   - Notice any changes in your thoughts or emotions.
4. **Reassess**:
   - Re-rate your distress. If it has decreased, continue for another 20–30 seconds. If it hasn't, shift your focus to a calming image or thought.

2. Safe Place Visualization

The safe place exercise is a calming technique often used in the preparation phase of E M D R therapy. It helps create a mental retreat where you can ground yourself during emotional distress.

Steps for Creating a Safe Place

1. **Find a Quiet Space**:
   - Sit comfortably and close your eyes.
2. **Visualize Your Safe Place**:

- Imagine a location where you feel completely at ease (e.g., a beach, forest, or cozy room). Make it as vivid as possible:
  - What do you see?
  - What do you hear?
  - What do you smell?
  - What do you feel (e.g., the warmth of the sun or a soft blanket)?

3. **Anchor the Feeling**:
   - Focus on the sense of peace and safety this place brings. Engage in gentle tapping on your knees or shoulders to enhance the calming effect.

4. **Practice Regularly**:
   - Revisit your safe place daily so that it becomes easier to access during moments of stress.

3. Reprocessing Negative Beliefs

Self-help E M D R can help you challenge and replace negative beliefs that contribute to stress or low self-esteem.

Steps for Reprocessing Negative Beliefs

1. **Identify the Negative Belief**:
   - Reflect on a specific situation where you felt upset. Ask yourself, "What negative belief about myself does this situation reinforce?" (e.g., "I'm not good enough").

2. **Choose a Positive Belief**:
   - Select a belief you'd like to internalize instead (e.g., "I am capable and worthy").

3. **Engage in BLS**:
   - Think about the negative belief while tapping alternately on your knees or following an object with your eyes. Notice any changes in how you feel.

4. **Shift to the Positive Belief**:

- Focus on your chosen positive belief while continuing BLS. Imagine yourself embodying this belief in a future scenario.

5. **Repeat Regularly**:
   - Practice this exercise whenever negative beliefs arise to reinforce a healthier mindset.

4. Managing Everyday Triggers

Triggers are reminders of past experiences that provoke emotional or physical reactions. Learning to identify and manage them is a key part of self-help E M D R.

Steps for Handling Triggers

1. **Identify the Trigger**:
   - Notice situations, people, or environments that cause you to feel anxious, upset, or on edge.
2. **Pause and Ground Yourself**:
   - Engage in a grounding technique, such as deep breathing or bilateral tapping, to calm your nervous system.
3. **Reframe the Trigger**:
   - Remind yourself that the trigger is not a threat. Say to yourself, "I am safe now" or "This is just a reminder, not the event itself."
4. **Reassess Your Reaction**:
   - Notice if your emotional intensity has decreased. If needed, return to your grounding techniques until you feel more centered.

5. Journaling with a Focus on E M D R Principles

Journaling is a powerful tool for self-reflection and emotional processing. Incorporating E M D R-inspired techniques into your journaling practice can enhance its effectiveness.

Steps for E M D R-Inspired Journaling

1. **Write About a Mildly Distressing Event**:
    - Describe the situation, your emotions, and any physical sensations you experienced.
2. **Identify Negative and Positive Beliefs**:
    - Write down the negative belief associated with the event (e.g., "I failed"), then identify a positive belief you'd like to hold instead (e.g., "I tried my best").
3. **Engage in BLS While Journaling**:
    - Alternate tapping on your knees or shoulders as you reflect on the event and reframe it with the positive belief.
4. **End with Gratitude**:
    - Conclude your entry by listing three things you're grateful for, shifting your focus to a positive state of mind.

6. Practicing Emotional Regulation Techniques

E M D R self-help techniques often integrate emotional regulation strategies to help manage distress in real time.

Techniques to Try

- **Tapping (EFT)**: Gently tap on specific acupressure points while repeating a calming phrase, such as "I am safe."
- **Butterfly Hug**: Cross your arms over your chest and alternately tap your shoulders in a soothing rhythm.
- **Box Breathing**: Inhale for four counts, hold for four counts, exhale for four counts, and hold for four counts. Repeat until you feel calm.

Benefits of Self-Help E M D R Techniques

1. **Empowerment**: These techniques allow you to take an active role in your emotional healing.

2. **Stress Reduction**: They provide immediate relief during moments of distress.
3. **Reinforcement of Therapy**: Self-help methods can reinforce progress made in professional E M D R sessions.
4. **Accessibility**: They can be practiced anytime, anywhere, without specialized equipment.

When to Seek Professional Support

While self-help E M D R techniques can be highly effective for everyday challenges, complex trauma and deeply ingrained patterns often require the guidance of a trained E M D R therapist. If you experience severe distress, intrusive memories, or feel overwhelmed during self-help exercises, reach out to a mental health professional.

What Readers Will Learn: Techniques for Managing Minor Anxieties and Emotional Blocks

While Eye Movement Desensitization and Reprocessing (E M D R) therapy is traditionally facilitated by a trained therapist, certain techniques inspired by E M D R principles can be adapted for personal use. These self-help techniques are especially useful for addressing **minor anxieties, emotional blocks, and everyday stressors**, empowering readers to take an active role in managing their emotional well-being. In this section, readers will learn practical, step-by-step methods they can use independently to find relief and build resilience.

1. The Butterfly Hug: A Calming Technique for Emotional Regulation

The Butterfly Hug is a simple yet powerful bilateral stimulation (BLS) technique designed to promote relaxation and calm during moments of stress or emotional discomfort.

Steps to Practice the Butterfly Hug

1. **Cross Your Arms Over Your Chest**:
   - Place your hands on opposite shoulders, forming a "butterfly" shape with your arms.
2. **Begin Gentle Tapping**:
   - Alternate tapping your shoulders with your hands in a slow, rhythmic motion.
3. **Focus on Your Breathing**:
   - Take deep breaths, inhaling for a count of four, holding for four, and exhaling for six.
4. **Reflect on a Positive Thought**:
   - Visualize a calming image, such as a serene beach or a warm, comforting memory.
5. **Continue Until Calm**:
   - Repeat the exercise for 1–2 minutes or until you feel more grounded.

When to Use It

- During moments of anxiety, such as before a presentation or difficult conversation.
- To calm yourself after a triggering event or stressful day.

2. Safe Place Visualization: Creating Your Inner Sanctuary

Safe Place Visualization is a guided imagery technique that helps establish a mental "retreat" to reduce anxiety and create a sense of security.

Steps to Create Your Safe Place

1. **Find a Quiet Spot**:
   - Sit or lie down in a comfortable position where you won't be disturbed.
2. **Visualize Your Safe Place**:

- Imagine a location where you feel completely at peace—this could be a beach, forest, cozy room, or garden.

3. **Engage Your Senses**:
   - What do you see, hear, feel, smell, or taste in this place? Make it as vivid as possible.
4. **Anchor the Feeling**:
   - Focus on the sense of calm this place brings. For added effectiveness, gently tap your knees or shoulders alternately while visualizing.
5. **Practice Regularly**:
   - Visit your safe place daily so it becomes a natural resource during moments of stress.

When to Use It

- Before bed to unwind and improve sleep quality.
- As a grounding exercise when dealing with mild anxiety or emotional overwhelm.

3. Tapping for Emotional Relief

Also known as Emotional Freedom Techniques (EFT), tapping involves gently stimulating specific acupressure points on the body while addressing a distressing emotion or thought.

Steps to Use Tapping

1. **Identify the Emotion or Thought**:
   - Choose a specific worry or block (e.g., "I feel anxious about tomorrow's meeting").
2. **Rate Your Distress**:
   - On a scale from 0 (no distress) to 10 (maximum distress), note how strongly you feel.
3. **Tap on Key Points**:
   - Use your fingers to tap gently on the following areas, repeating your thought aloud:

- The side of your hand (karate chop point).
- Top of your head.
- Inner eyebrow.
- Side of the eye.
- Under the eye.
- Under the nose.
- Chin.
- Collarbone.
- Underarm.

4. **Reassess Your Distress**:
   - After a few rounds, re-rate your distress. Repeat until the intensity decreases.

When to Use It

- To address immediate worries or mild anxieties.
- As a daily practice to release minor emotional tension.

4. Reprocessing Minor Emotional Blocks

This E M D R-inspired technique allows you to work through smaller emotional challenges or mental blocks on your own, helping to shift your perspective and reduce stress.

Steps for Self-Reprocessing

1. **Identify a Minor Block**:
   - Choose a mild issue, such as procrastination, fear of speaking up, or feeling stuck on a small decision.
2. **Focus on the Negative Belief**:
   - Identify the negative thought associated with the block (e.g., "I'm not good at this").
3. **Engage in Bilateral Stimulation**:
   - Use tapping, eye movements, or alternating tones to stimulate both sides of your brain while focusing on the negative belief.
4. **Shift to a Positive Belief**:

- Replace the negative thought with a more empowering one (e.g., "I am capable of learning this").

5. **Reassess Your Emotional Intensity**:
   - Notice if the belief feels less "true" or intense after the exercise. Repeat as needed.

When to Use It

- When facing small but recurring doubts or fears.
- To shift mental energy before tackling a task.

5. Journaling for Emotional Clarity

Incorporating E M D R principles into your journaling practice can help process minor anxieties and clarify emotions.

Steps for E M D R-Inspired Journaling

1. **Write About the Issue**:
   - Describe the situation or feeling that's causing mild anxiety.
2. **Identify Beliefs and Emotions**:
   - Note any negative beliefs or emotions tied to the issue.
3. **Reframe with Positive Beliefs**:
   - Write down a positive belief you'd like to adopt instead.
4. **Engage in Bilateral Stimulation**:
   - While journaling, gently tap your knees or shoulders alternately, allowing thoughts and emotions to flow.
5. **End with Gratitude**:
   - Close your entry with three things you're grateful for to shift your focus to a positive mindset.

When to Use It

- To process emotions after a stressful day.
- As a morning practice to start the day with clarity and focus.

6. Bilateral Breathing for Calmness

Combining breathing exercises with BLS can amplify their calming effect, helping to reduce anxiety and regain focus.

Steps for Bilateral Breathing

1. **Sit Comfortably**:
   - Place your feet flat on the ground and rest your hands on your knees.
2. **Engage in BLS**:
   - Tap alternately on your knees with your hands in a slow rhythm.
3. **Focus on Your Breath**:
   - Inhale for four counts, hold for four counts, and exhale for six counts.
4. **Combine Both Actions**:
   - Maintain the tapping while focusing on your breath for 2–3 minutes.

When to Use It

- Before entering a potentially stressful situation, such as a meeting or presentation.
- To calm your nerves during unexpected moments of anxiety.

Why These Techniques Work

The self-help techniques in this chapter are rooted in E M D R's core principles of **bilateral stimulation**, **cognitive reframing**, and **grounding**. By engaging both hemispheres of the brain, these methods promote emotional balance, reduce stress, and help process minor issues without becoming overwhelmed. Regular practice of these techniques can build resilience, making it easier to handle everyday challenges.

Why It Stands Out: A Focus on Safe Self-Practice Exercises Tailored for Non-Therapist-Guided Use

This book stands out because it empowers readers to take control of their emotional well-being through safe, effective, and **therapist-free self-practice exercises** inspired by the principles of Eye Movement Desensitization and Reprocessing (E M D R). These techniques are carefully designed to address minor emotional challenges, promote emotional regulation, and reduce stress without the risks associated with unstructured trauma work. The focus on safety, accessibility, and simplicity makes these exercises a valuable tool for anyone seeking relief from anxiety, emotional blocks, or daily stressors.

The Importance of Safety in Self-Practice

Engaging in self-guided E M D R-inspired exercises requires a focus on safety, especially when dealing with emotional memories. Unlike traditional E M D R therapy facilitated by a licensed therapist, these self-practice techniques are tailored to avoid deep trauma processing, ensuring that readers can:

- Safely manage mild emotional distress without risking emotional overwhelm.
- Develop tools for everyday stress relief and resilience-building.
- Reinforce progress made during professional therapy.

How These Exercises Are Designed for Safety

1. Targeting Mild Emotional Challenges

- The self-practice exercises focus on **low-intensity stressors or emotional blocks** rather than severe trauma.
- Readers are guided to assess their emotional state before starting, ensuring they stay within a manageable range of distress.

2. Gradual and Reversible Techniques

- Each exercise emphasizes **gradual progress**, allowing readers to pause or stop if emotions become too intense.
- The book provides clear instructions on returning to a calm state through grounding techniques or safe place visualizations.

3. Built-In Stabilization Tools

- Readers are equipped with **stabilization techniques** such as deep breathing, progressive muscle relaxation, and positive imagery to maintain emotional balance before, during, and after exercises.

4. Clear Boundaries

- The book explicitly advises against attempting to process **deep trauma or unresolved grief** without professional guidance.
- Readers are encouraged to seek professional help if exercises trigger intense emotions or memories.

Examples of Safe Self-Practice Exercises

The following exercises are tailored for non-therapist-guided use, focusing on manageable emotional challenges and promoting emotional well-being

1. Bilateral Tapping for Everyday Stress

Bilateral tapping is a simple and effective method for calming the nervous system and managing everyday anxiety.

Steps:

1. Sit in a comfortable position and place your hands on your knees.
2. Begin tapping your knees alternately—left, then right—in a slow, rhythmic motion.
3. Focus on your breathing: inhale for four counts, hold for four, and exhale for six.
4. Think about a mildly distressing situation (e.g., feeling overwhelmed at work) while tapping.
5. Continue for 1–2 minutes, then reflect on whether the intensity of your distress has decreased.

Why It's Safe:

- This exercise targets low-level stressors, making it suitable for self-practice.
- Readers can stop tapping at any time and shift their focus to a calming image or thought.

2. Safe Place Visualization for Emotional Grounding

The safe place exercise helps create a mental retreat that readers can return to during moments of emotional discomfort.

Steps:

1. Close your eyes and imagine a location where you feel completely at peace (e.g., a quiet forest, a cozy room).
2. Engage your senses: What does this place look like? What sounds do you hear? How does it feel to be there?
3. While visualizing, gently tap your shoulders or knees alternately for 1–2 minutes.

4. Anchor the feeling of safety by repeating a calming phrase, such as "I am safe and at peace."

Why It's Safe:

- The exercise is non-triggering and focuses solely on creating a sense of calm.
- It can be practiced anywhere, making it a versatile tool for managing stress.

3. Reframing Negative Thoughts with Positive Beliefs

This exercise helps readers shift their mindset by replacing negative self-talk with empowering beliefs.

Steps:

1. Identify a mildly negative thought (e.g., "I'm not good enough").
2. Write down a positive belief to replace it (e.g., "I am capable and deserving of success").
3. While focusing on the negative thought, begin bilateral tapping or follow an object moving side to side.
4. Shift your focus to the positive belief and repeat it aloud or silently while continuing the tapping.
5. Repeat for 1–2 minutes, then pause and reflect on any changes in your emotional state.

Why It's Safe:

- The exercise stays within the realm of cognitive reframing, avoiding deep emotional triggers.
- Readers can focus on small, specific challenges, ensuring the process feels manageable.

4. Butterfly Hug for Self-Soothing

The Butterfly Hug is a gentle BLS technique that promotes emotional regulation and relaxation.

Steps:

1. Cross your arms over your chest, placing your hands on opposite shoulders.
2. Tap your shoulders alternately in a slow, rhythmic motion.
3. Focus on your breathing: inhale deeply through your nose, hold for a moment, and exhale slowly through your mouth.
4. Reflect on a positive memory or calming image while continuing the tapping.
5. Continue for as long as needed to feel grounded.

Why It's Safe:

- The Butterfly Hug is simple, non-intrusive, and easy to practice without external guidance.
- It focuses on calming rather than reprocessing, making it ideal for self-help.

5. Emotional Check-In with Journaling

Journaling provides a safe space for reflecting on emotions and identifying patterns of thought or behavior.

Steps:

1. Set aside 10 minutes in a quiet space.
2. Write down how you're feeling and any specific situations that contributed to those emotions.
3. Identify any negative beliefs associated with these feelings and write them down.

4. End by reframing the negative beliefs into positive affirmations and focusing on gratitude (e.g., "I am learning and growing").
5. Use bilateral tapping while rereading your affirmations to reinforce them.

Why It's Safe:

- Journaling allows readers to process emotions at their own pace without external pressure.
- Combining it with bilateral tapping adds an extra layer of emotional support.

Empowering Readers with Self-Practice

This book's focus on safe self-practice exercises empowers readers by:

1. **Building Emotional Resilience**: These techniques provide tools to handle everyday stress and challenges independently.
2. **Fostering Emotional Awareness**: Exercises like journaling and visualization encourage introspection and self-understanding.
3. **Promoting Self-Reliance**: Readers gain confidence in managing their emotions without always relying on external support.
4. **Complementing Professional Therapy**: These exercises reinforce therapeutic progress, helping readers maintain emotional balance between sessions.

Chapter 6: E M D R for Different Types of Trauma

Eye Movement Desensitization and Reprocessing (E M D R) therapy is a transformative method designed to address the lingering effects of trauma. One of its greatest strengths lies in its versatility: it can effectively treat a wide range of traumatic experiences, from acute, one-time events to chronic, complex patterns of distress. By tailoring its structured, eight-phase approach to the specific needs of the individual, E M D R provides a powerful tool for healing and recovery across diverse types of trauma.

In this chapter, readers will learn how E M D R is adapted to address different categories of trauma, complete with examples and insights into why it is particularly effective for each type.

1. Acute Trauma

Acute trauma stems from a single, distressing event, such as an accident, natural disaster, or sudden loss. These experiences often leave a lasting emotional impact, even if they occur just once.

How E M D R Works for Acute Trauma

- E M D R helps desensitize the emotional intensity of the memory by reprocessing it and integrating it into a neutral narrative.
- Bilateral stimulation (BLS) engages both hemispheres of the brain, promoting the natural processing of fragmented memories.
- Positive beliefs, such as "I am safe now," replace negative beliefs, such as "I am in danger."

Example: Healing from a Car Accident

- **Client Profile**: Alex, a 34-year-old graphic designer, experienced panic attacks after a car crash.
- **E M D R Process**:
    - **Assessment**: Alex's target memory was the moment of impact during the accident.
    - **Desensitization**: With BLS, the memory's emotional charge diminished, and Alex began to feel that the crash was in the past, not an ongoing threat.
    - **Installation**: Alex replaced the belief "I am unsafe" with "I can drive confidently."

Outcome: After several sessions, Alex was able to drive without fear and regained control over his life.

2. Chronic Trauma

Chronic trauma results from prolonged exposure to distressing situations, such as ongoing abuse, bullying, or living in a dangerous environment. Unlike acute trauma, chronic trauma often involves repeated violations of safety and trust.

How E M D R Works for Chronic Trauma

- E M D R addresses the cumulative impact of repeated stress by targeting multiple interconnected memories and beliefs.
- Therapy often progresses gradually, starting with less distressing memories to build emotional resilience before tackling more intense experiences.

Example: Recovering from Workplace Harassment

- **Client Profile**: Sarah, a 40-year-old nurse, suffered from years of verbal abuse by a supervisor, leading to low self-esteem and anxiety.

- **E M D R Process**:
  - **Assessment**: Sarah identified a series of incidents where she felt belittled.
  - **Desensitization**: Each memory was reprocessed, reducing its emotional intensity.
  - **Installation**: Positive beliefs like "I am competent and valuable" replaced negative self-perceptions.

Outcome: Sarah gained confidence, set boundaries, and pursued a healthier work environment.

3. Complex Trauma

Complex trauma involves prolonged, severe harm, often beginning in childhood. It includes experiences like neglect, emotional or physical abuse, and exposure to unstable caregiving environments.

How E M D R Works for Complex Trauma

- E M D R is used carefully and incrementally to avoid overwhelming the individual.
- The safe place visualization and grounding techniques are heavily emphasized to build emotional stability.
- Therapy often involves working on foundational memories that contribute to maladaptive patterns.

Example: Healing Childhood Neglect

- **Client Profile**: David, a 28-year-old IT professional, struggled with trust issues and emotional numbness stemming from neglect in his early years.
- **E M D R Process**:
  - **Preparation**: David practiced grounding exercises to manage emotional intensity.
  - **Desensitization**: Memories of being left alone for hours as a child were reprocessed,

helping him move from "I am invisible" to "I am worthy of attention."

- **Body Scan**: Physical tension in his chest released as he processed these memories.

Outcome: Over time, David developed healthier relationships and felt more connected to his emotions.

4. P T S D from Combat or Violent Events

Post-Traumatic Stress Disorder (P T S D) often develops in individuals who have experienced or witnessed life-threatening events, such as combat, physical assault, or violent crime.

How E M D R Works for P T S D

- E M D R directly addresses the vivid, intrusive memories that characterize P T S D.
- By reprocessing the traumatic memory, E M D R reduces flashbacks, nightmares, and hypervigilance.

Example: A Veteran's Recovery

- **Client Profile**: James, a 45-year-old veteran, experienced debilitating flashbacks of combat.
- **E M D R Process**:
    - **Assessment**: The memory of a specific ambush was identified as the primary target.
    - **Desensitization**: BLS helped James reduce the memory's intensity, allowing him to recall it without reliving it.
    - **Installation**: James replaced the belief "I am helpless" with "I am strong and capable."

Outcome: James regained a sense of safety and began engaging in daily life without fear.

5. Trauma from Grief and Loss

Trauma can arise from the death of a loved one or other significant losses, such as divorce or job termination. While grief is a natural response, unresolved trauma can complicate the healing process.

How E M D R Works for Grief and Loss

- E M D R helps process the pain associated with the loss, reducing feelings of guilt, regret, or anger.
- It allows individuals to focus on positive memories of the lost person or situation, fostering acceptance and emotional peace.

Example: Coping with the Loss of a Parent

- **Client Profile**: Priya, a 30-year-old teacher, felt overwhelming guilt after the sudden death of her mother, believing she could have done more.
- **E M D R Process**:
    - **Desensitization**: Priya processed memories of her mother's final days, letting go of guilt and regret.
    - **Installation**: Positive beliefs like "I did my best" and "My mother knew I loved her" were reinforced.

Outcome: Priya began to cherish her memories with her mother without being overwhelmed by guilt.

6. Phobias and Specific Fears

Phobias, such as fear of flying or public speaking, often stem from past negative experiences. While not always linked to trauma, these fears can significantly disrupt daily life.

How E M D R Works for Phobias

- E M D R uncovers and reprocesses the root cause of the fear, whether it's a specific memory or a generalized sense of threat.
- Positive beliefs replace the negative associations tied to the phobia.

Example: Overcoming Fear of Flying

- **Client Profile**: Laura, a 27-year-old consultant, avoided flights due to a turbulent experience years ago.
- **E M D R Process**:
    - **Desensitization**: Laura processed the memory of the turbulence using BLS, reducing her fear response.
    - **Installation**: She internalized the belief "Flying is safe and manageable."

Outcome: Laura began flying confidently for work and leisure.

7. Trauma from Medical Procedures or Illness

Medical trauma can arise from invasive procedures, misdiagnoses, or prolonged illnesses, leaving individuals with anxiety or a fear of healthcare settings.

How E M D R Works for Medical Trauma

- E M D R helps desensitize distressing memories of medical experiences.
- It reduces anticipatory anxiety about future procedures or appointments.

Example: Processing a Traumatic Surgery

- **Client Profile**: Michael, a 50-year-old chef, developed panic attacks after a painful surgery.

- **E M D R Process**:
  - **Assessment**: The memory of waking up in post-operative pain was targeted.
  - **Desensitization**: Michael processed the memory with BLS, reducing its emotional charge.
  - **Installation**: He adopted the belief "I can handle medical care."

Outcome: Michael regained trust in medical professionals and felt prepared for future check-ups.

Why E M D R Is Effective for Different Types of Trauma

1. **Tailored Approach**: E M D R's structured phases allow for customization based on the type and intensity of trauma.
2. **Holistic Healing**: E M D R addresses emotional, cognitive, and physical aspects of trauma, providing comprehensive relief.
3. **Efficient and Lasting Results**: Many individuals experience significant improvement in fewer sessions compared to traditional talk therapy.

What Readers Will Learn: How E M D R Can Address Different Types of Trauma

E M D R (Eye Movement Desensitization and Reprocessing) therapy is a powerful, science-backed approach to trauma healing that adapts to a wide range of traumatic experiences. Readers will learn how E M D R can be effectively applied to address diverse types of trauma, including childhood trauma, grief, accidents, and complex P T S D. Each type of trauma carries unique challenges, but E M D R's structured eight-phase framework offers a tailored path to relief and recovery. This section provides an in-depth exploration of how E M D R addresses each category of trauma, highlighting the therapy's versatility and transformative potential.

1. Childhood Trauma

Childhood trauma often involves neglect, abuse, or unstable caregiving environments. These experiences can leave a lasting imprint on emotional regulation, self-esteem, and relationships, persisting into adulthood as unresolved wounds.

How E M D R Helps with Childhood Trauma

- **Reprocessing Foundational Memories**: E M D R targets early memories that shaped negative beliefs (e.g., "I am unlovable") and helps replace them with positive beliefs (e.g., "I am worthy of love").
- **Building Emotional Safety**: Through techniques like safe place visualization, E M D R fosters a sense of safety and security, essential for processing painful childhood experiences.
- **Addressing Attachment Issues**: E M D R can address difficulties in forming healthy relationships stemming from insecure attachments during childhood.

Example Scenario

Maria's Story: Maria, a 32-year-old professional, experienced neglect as a child, leaving her feeling unworthy and emotionally distant in relationships. Through E M D R, Maria processed memories of being left alone and reframed her self-perception, adopting the belief, "I am deserving of care and connection." Over time, Maria developed healthier relationships and a stronger sense of self-worth.

2. Grief and Loss

Trauma from grief and loss often arises from the sudden death of a loved one, divorce, or other significant separations. These events can lead to complicated grief, where unresolved emotions like guilt or regret prevent healing.

How E M D R Helps with Grief

- **Processing Painful Memories**: E M D R helps reprocess distressing moments, such as the final days of a loved one or a traumatic breakup, reducing emotional intensity.
- **Letting Go of Guilt**: Many individuals feel guilt or responsibility for events outside their control. E M D R addresses these emotions, fostering acceptance and peace.
- **Focusing on Positive Memories**: Once the pain is desensitized, E M D R can strengthen positive memories and beliefs, helping individuals cherish what they've lost without being overwhelmed by sadness.

Example Scenario

John's Story: John lost his wife unexpectedly and struggled with guilt, believing he hadn't done enough to save her. E M D R helped John reprocess his memories, replacing the belief "I failed her" with "I loved her and did my best." This shift allowed John to move forward with a sense of peace and gratitude for their time together.

3. Accidents and Acute Trauma

Accidents, natural disasters, and sudden violent events can leave individuals with lingering fear, panic, or phobias. These experiences often manifest as acute trauma or Post-Traumatic Stress Disorder (P T S D).

How E M D R Helps with Accidents and Acute Trauma

- **Desensitizing Flashbacks**: E M D R reduces the emotional intensity of distressing memories, such as the moment of an impact or a sudden explosion.
- **Replacing Fear with Confidence**: Negative beliefs like "I am unsafe" are replaced with empowering beliefs like "I can navigate challenges."
- **Restoring a Sense of Normalcy**: E M D R helps individuals view the traumatic event as part of the past, reducing its influence on daily life.

Example Scenario

Lisa's Story: Lisa, a 29-year-old architect, developed a fear of driving after a car accident. Through E M D R, she reprocessed the memory of the accident, reduced her fear response, and internalized the belief, "I can drive safely and confidently." Lisa regained her independence and resumed her daily activities without fear.

4. Complex P T S D

Complex P T S D develops from prolonged exposure to trauma, often involving multiple events over time. It frequently includes emotional abuse, repeated violations of safety or trust, and chronic neglect.

How E M D R Helps with Complex P T S D

- **Step-by-Step Healing**: E M D R tackles complex trauma incrementally, starting with less distressing memories to build resilience before addressing core traumatic events.
- **Rebuilding Self-Worth**: E M D R challenges deeply ingrained beliefs like "I am broken" or "I am powerless," replacing them with positive affirmations.

- **Integrating Fragmented Experiences**: Complex trauma often results in fragmented memories. E M D R helps integrate these pieces into a cohesive, less overwhelming narrative.

Example Scenario

David's Story: David, a 40-year-old entrepreneur, endured years of emotional abuse from his parents. He felt stuck in patterns of self-doubt and emotional isolation. E M D R allowed him to process key moments of his abuse and adopt a new belief: "I am strong and deserving of love." This transformation helped David establish boundaries and build healthier relationships.

5. Combat and Violent Events

Combat veterans and survivors of violent events often experience P T S D symptoms like hypervigilance, flashbacks, and emotional numbness. These symptoms can severely disrupt daily life.

How E M D R Helps with Combat and Violence Trauma

- **Reducing Intrusive Symptoms**: E M D R helps desensitize intrusive memories, reducing their emotional and sensory intensity.
- **Restoring a Sense of Safety**: Through reprocessing, E M D R reinforces beliefs like "I am safe now" or "I can protect myself."
- **Promoting Emotional Connection**: E M D R helps individuals reconnect with their emotions, fostering healthier relationships and improved quality of life.

Example Scenario

James's Story: James, a 35-year-old combat veteran, struggled with nightmares and flashbacks of an ambush. E M D R helped James reprocess the memory, reducing its intensity, and adopt the belief, "I am safe in the present." James regained control over his life, reconnecting with his family and finding peace.

Why E M D R Works Across Different Types of Trauma

- **Customizable Approach**: The eight-phase framework of E M D R allows therapists to tailor treatment to specific needs, whether it's a single incident or years of compounded trauma.
- **Holistic Healing**: E M D R addresses the emotional, cognitive, and physical dimensions of trauma, providing comprehensive relief.
- **Effective Across Ages and Backgrounds**: From childhood trauma to adult grief, E M D R adapts to individuals of all ages and experiences, making it widely applicable.

What Readers Will Gain

By learning how E M D R addresses various types of trauma, readers will:

- Understand how tailored E M D R approaches can provide relief from childhood trauma, grief, accidents, and complex P T S D.
- Gain insight into how trauma impacts emotions, beliefs, and behaviors, and how E M D R transforms those patterns.
- Feel empowered to explore E M D R as a healing option for their unique experiences or recommend it to loved ones in need.

Why It Stands Out: Offers Specific Examples of Each Trauma Type and Practical Solutions for Each

This book stands out because it provides detailed, real-world examples for various types of trauma, coupled with practical, E M D R-inspired solutions tailored to address each unique experience. By breaking down each trauma type and illustrating how E M D R techniques can be applied, readers gain a clear understanding of how they or their loved ones can use these approaches for healing. This combination of relatable scenarios and actionable steps ensures that the concepts are accessible, empowering readers to take meaningful steps toward recovery.

1. Childhood Trauma

Childhood trauma often stems from abuse, neglect, or unstable environments. Its effects can persist into adulthood, influencing self-esteem, relationships, and emotional regulation.

Example: Healing Childhood Neglect

- **Scenario**: Maria grew up feeling invisible in her household, as her parents were emotionally unavailable. This led to feelings of unworthiness and difficulty forming close relationships.
- **E M D R Solution**:
    - **Target Memory**: Maria focuses on memories of being ignored, reprocessing them through bilateral stimulation (BLS).
    - **Negative Belief**: "I am unworthy of love."
    - **Positive Belief**: "I am deserving of love and attention."
    - **Practical Exercise**: Maria practices a **safe place visualization**, imagining a nurturing environment where she feels seen and valued.

This becomes her emotional anchor during moments of self-doubt.

2. Grief and Loss

Grief becomes traumatic when unresolved emotions, such as guilt or regret, prevent the natural healing process. E M D R can help individuals process painful memories and accept their loss.

Example: Coping with the Loss of a Loved One

- **Scenario**: John lost his mother suddenly and struggles with guilt, believing he didn't spend enough time with her.
- **E M D R Solution**:
    - **Target Memory**: John reprocesses his last interaction with his mother, reducing the emotional charge associated with it.
    - **Negative Belief**: "I didn't do enough."
    - **Positive Belief**: "I showed my love in the time we had."
    - **Practical Exercise**: John writes a letter to his mother expressing his feelings, followed by bilateral tapping as he reflects on positive memories. This helps him shift his focus from guilt to gratitude.

3. Accidents and Acute Trauma

Trauma from accidents or sudden, distressing events can leave individuals with heightened fear, avoidance behaviors, and intrusive memories.

Example: Recovering from a Car Accident

- **Scenario**: Lisa avoids driving after a car accident, experiencing panic attacks at the thought of being behind the wheel.

- **E M D R Solution**:
  - **Target Memory**: Lisa focuses on the moment of impact, using BLS to reduce its emotional intensity.
  - **Negative Belief**: "I am unsafe on the road."
  - **Positive Belief**: "I can drive safely and confidently."
  - **Practical Exercise**: Lisa practices **bilateral breathing** (tapping while focusing on her breath) before driving short distances. Gradually, she expands her comfort zone, integrating the belief, "I am in control."

4. Complex P T S D

Complex P T S D arises from prolonged exposure to trauma, often involving multiple events. It frequently results in fragmented memories, emotional dysregulation, and negative core beliefs.

Example: Addressing Emotional Abuse

- **Scenario**: David, a 38-year-old software developer, endured years of emotional abuse from a parent. He struggles with feelings of inadequacy and fear of criticism.
- **E M D R Solution**:
  - **Target Memories**: David works on specific incidents of verbal abuse, processing them through BLS.
  - **Negative Belief**: "I am not good enough."
  - **Positive Belief**: "I am capable and deserving of respect."
  - **Practical Exercise**: David practices **journaling with bilateral stimulation**, rewriting his self-perception by focusing on positive affirmations and moments where he demonstrated resilience.

5. Combat and Violent Events

Combat veterans and survivors of violent incidents often experience flashbacks, hypervigilance, and emotional numbness. These symptoms can disrupt daily functioning and relationships.

Example: Healing Combat Trauma

- **Scenario**: James, a retired soldier, experiences flashbacks from an ambush during deployment. Loud noises trigger his anxiety, making daily life challenging.
- **E M D R Solution**:
    - **Target Memory**: James processes the memory of the ambush, desensitizing its intensity through BLS.
    - **Negative Belief**: "I am in danger."
    - **Positive Belief**: "I am safe now."
    - **Practical Exercise**: James uses the **Butterfly Hug** technique during moments of hypervigilance, reminding himself of his positive belief: "The danger is in the past."

6. Phobias and Specific Fears

Phobias, such as fear of flying or public speaking, often stem from past negative experiences or perceived threats. These fears can significantly disrupt daily life but are highly treatable with E M D R.

Example: Overcoming Fear of Public Speaking

- **Scenario**: Priya avoids presentations at work due to a humiliating experience in high school.
- **E M D R Solution**:
    - **Target Memory**: Priya reprocesses the memory of being laughed at during a class speech.

- **Negative Belief**: "I will fail and embarrass myself."
- **Positive Belief**: "I can speak confidently and connect with my audience."
- **Practical Exercise**: Priya practices her speech while engaging in **bilateral tapping**, focusing on her positive belief. This reduces anticipatory anxiety and reinforces confidence.

7. Medical Trauma

Medical trauma can result from invasive procedures, misdiagnoses, or prolonged illness, leaving individuals with fear or distrust of healthcare settings.

Example: Processing Trauma from Surgery

- **Scenario**: Michael, a 50-year-old chef, avoids hospitals after a traumatic surgery where he experienced unexpected pain.
- **E M D R Solution**:
    - **Target Memory**: Michael focuses on the memory of waking up in pain and reprocesses it with BLS.
    - **Negative Belief**: "I can't trust doctors."
    - **Positive Belief**: "I can advocate for myself and trust the care I receive."
    - **Practical Exercise**: Michael uses **safe place visualization** before medical appointments to reduce anxiety, imagining himself in a comforting environment.

How These Examples Empower Readers

- **Relatability**: Real-world scenarios help readers see themselves in the stories, fostering a sense of connection and hope.
- **Clarity**: By breaking down how E M D R targets specific types of trauma, readers gain a deeper

understanding of the therapy's adaptability and effectiveness.

- **Actionable Insights**: Practical solutions offer readers immediate tools to address minor issues or prepare for professional E M D R therapy.
- **Motivation**: Success stories inspire readers to seek E M D R as a pathway to healing, showing that recovery is possible regardless of the trauma type.

Chapter 7: E M D R for Everyday Stress and Anxiety

While Eye Movement Desensitization and Reprocessing (E M D R) is best known for addressing trauma, its principles can also be applied to manage everyday stress and anxiety. These techniques provide powerful tools for calming the nervous system, reframing negative thoughts, and building resilience in the face of daily challenges. This chapter explores how E M D R-inspired practices can be adapted for non-therapist-guided use to help individuals navigate common stressors and maintain emotional balance.

Why E M D R Is Effective for Everyday Stress and Anxiety

- **Dual Action**: E M D R engages both hemispheres of the brain, helping to regulate emotional responses and integrate new, more positive beliefs.
- **Calms the Nervous System**: Bilateral stimulation (BLS) reduces physiological stress responses, making it easier to face challenges with a clear mind.
- **Builds Resilience**: Reprocessing minor stressors trains the brain to respond more calmly to future triggers.

1. Using E M D R for Work-Related Stress

Workplace stress can stem from tight deadlines, conflicts, or performance pressures. These stressors often trigger negative beliefs about competence or worth.

Example Scenario

- **Scenario**: Maya, a 28-year-old marketing professional, feels overwhelmed by her growing workload. She often tells herself, "I can't handle this."
- **E M D R Solution**:

- **Target Stressor**: Maya focuses on a specific moment, such as feeling overwhelmed while reviewing a long to-do list.
- **Negative Belief**: "I am not capable."
- **Positive Belief**: "I can prioritize and handle challenges."
- **Practical Exercise**: Maya uses bilateral tapping while visualizing herself completing one task at a time. As she continues, she feels more in control.

2. E M D R for Social Anxiety

Social situations can provoke feelings of self-doubt or fear of judgment, leading to avoidance behaviors.

Example Scenario

- **Scenario**: Priya avoids attending social events because she fears embarrassing herself in conversations.
- **E M D R Solution**:
  - **Target Stressor**: Priya recalls a recent social situation where she felt anxious, such as fumbling over her words.
  - **Negative Belief**: "I always say the wrong thing."
  - **Positive Belief**: "I can connect with others confidently."
  - **Practical Exercise**: Priya practices **butterfly tapping** while imagining herself in a positive social interaction. This exercise reduces her anxiety and reinforces self-assurance.

3. Managing Parental Stress

Parenting often comes with feelings of guilt, frustration, or worry about doing "enough" for your children.

Example Scenario

- **Scenario**: Sarah, a mother of two, feels guilty for losing her temper during a stressful morning routine.
- **E M D R Solution**:
  - **Target Stressor**: Sarah reprocesses the memory of her reaction, reducing the emotional charge tied to it.
  - **Negative Belief**: "I am a bad parent."
  - **Positive Belief**: "I am doing my best, and I can improve."
  - **Practical Exercise**: Sarah uses **safe place visualization** to calm herself after stressful mornings, imagining a serene beach where she feels patient and capable.

4. Handling Anxiety About the Future

Worries about the unknown, such as financial uncertainty or health concerns, can create persistent anxiety.

Example Scenario

- **Scenario**: James constantly feels on edge about upcoming bills and financial decisions.
- **E M D R Solution**:
  - **Target Stressor**: James focuses on his anxiety about paying the next bill, identifying the worst-case scenario in his mind.
  - **Negative Belief**: "I am helpless."
  - **Positive Belief**: "I can plan and take control of my finances."
  - **Practical Exercise**: James practices **bilateral breathing**, combining rhythmic tapping with deep breaths. This helps him reframe his worry as manageable.

5. Dealing with Minor Conflicts

Everyday disagreements, whether at home or work, can create lingering tension and negative emotions.

Example Scenario

- **Scenario**: Lisa feels hurt after an argument with her partner, replaying the event in her mind and thinking, "I can never say the right thing."
- **E M D R Solution**:
    - **Target Stressor**: Lisa focuses on the specific argument and the emotions tied to it.
    - **Negative Belief**: "I always mess up."
    - **Positive Belief**: "I can communicate effectively and resolve conflicts."
    - **Practical Exercise**: Lisa journals about the disagreement while engaging in bilateral tapping, helping her release the tension and approach her partner with a clearer mindset.

6. Managing Daily Overwhelm

The cumulative effect of small stressors—traffic, deadlines, or household chores—can lead to feelings of overwhelm.

Example Scenario

- **Scenario**: Emily feels paralyzed by her growing to-do list and struggles to know where to start.
- **E M D R Solution**:
    - **Target Stressor**: Emily focuses on her feelings of overwhelm while staring at her unfinished tasks.
    - **Negative Belief**: "I can't do this."
    - **Positive Belief**: "I can take it one step at a time."
    - **Practical Exercise**: Emily uses **tapping with visualization**, imagining herself calmly

completing each task. This shifts her mindset from panic to productivity.

7. Sleep Disruptions from Worry

Persistent worry can interfere with sleep, creating a cycle of stress and exhaustion.

Example Scenario

- **Scenario**: Mark lies awake replaying a conversation at work, worrying he offended a colleague.
- **E M D R Solution**:
    - **Target Stressor**: Mark focuses on the conversation and his fear of being judged.
    - **Negative Belief**: "I always make mistakes."
    - **Positive Belief**: "I can address this calmly tomorrow."
    - **Practical Exercise**: Mark practices **safe place visualization** paired with bilateral breathing, which soothes his nervous system and prepares his mind for restful sleep.

How Readers Can Apply E M D R for Stress

1. **Recognize Stress Patterns**:
    - Identify the situations or triggers that cause recurring stress or anxiety.
2. **Engage in Bilateral Stimulation (BLS)**:
    - Use techniques like tapping, alternating tones, or eye movements to process the associated emotions.
3. **Reframe Negative Beliefs**:
    - Replace self-defeating thoughts with empowering beliefs to shift your perspective.
4. **Incorporate Grounding Techniques**:
    - Use safe place visualization or bilateral breathing to anchor yourself in the present moment.

Why E M D R Works for Everyday Stress

- **Non-Invasive and Accessible**: E M D R-inspired exercises are easy to learn and implement at home or on the go.
- **Immediate Relief**: Techniques like tapping and safe place visualization can quickly reduce stress and anxiety in real-time.
- **Cumulative Benefits**: Regular practice builds emotional resilience, making it easier to manage future stressors.

What Readers Will Learn: Techniques for Managing Everyday Stress and Anxiety Using E M D R Principles

Readers will discover practical, E M D R-inspired techniques to tackle the challenges of everyday stress and anxiety. These methods, grounded in the principles of Eye Movement Desensitization and Reprocessing (E M D R), provide accessible, non-invasive tools for calming the mind, reframing negative beliefs, and building emotional resilience. Whether dealing with workplace pressures, relationship conflicts, or general anxiety, these techniques help regulate emotions and create a sense of control and balance in daily life.

1. Recognizing and Targeting Everyday Stressors

Understanding how to pinpoint the specific sources of stress is the first step in managing it. Readers will learn to:

- **Identify Triggers**: Recognize common stressors, such as tight deadlines, disagreements, or social obligations.
- **Break Down the Problem**: Focus on one specific moment or situation that feels manageable to address.

- **Assess Emotional Intensity**: Use a simple 0–10 scale to rate the level of stress or anxiety, ensuring the issue is mild enough for self-guided practice.

Example: A reader feeling overwhelmed by a long to-do list can identify the moment they became stressed, such as when they received an unexpected work assignment.

2. Bilateral Stimulation (BLS) for Emotional Regulation

BLS is the cornerstone of E M D R and involves engaging both hemispheres of the brain to reduce emotional intensity. Readers will learn various self-applied BLS techniques, including:

- **Tapping**: Alternately tap on the left and right knees, shoulders, or hands while focusing on the stressful situation.
- **Eye Movements**: Follow the movement of a pen, finger, or object side-to-side.
- **Auditory Stimulation**: Use headphones to listen to tones that alternate between the left and right ears.

How It Helps:

- BLS reduces the intensity of negative emotions and fosters a sense of calm.
- It mimics the natural processing that occurs during REM sleep, helping to reframe the way the brain perceives the stressor.

3. Reframing Negative Beliefs

Stress often triggers negative self-perceptions, such as "I can't handle this" or "I'm not good enough." E M D R-inspired techniques teach readers to:

- **Identify Negative Beliefs**: Recognize thoughts that amplify anxiety or self-doubt.
- **Create Positive Reframes**: Replace negative beliefs with empowering statements, such as "I can break this into smaller steps" or "I am capable."
- **Anchor Positive Beliefs with BLS**: Engage in tapping or eye movements while focusing on the positive belief to reinforce its impact.

Example: A reader stressed about an upcoming presentation might reframe "I will embarrass myself" into "I can prepare and speak confidently."

4. Safe Place Visualization for Grounding

The safe place technique provides a mental retreat where readers can feel calm and secure during moments of stress.

Steps to Practice Safe Place Visualization:

1. **Choose a Location**: Imagine a peaceful place, such as a beach, forest, or favorite childhood spot.
2. **Engage the Senses**: Picture the sights, sounds, smells, and physical sensations associated with this location.
3. **Pair with BLS**: While visualizing, gently tap alternately on your knees or shoulders to deepen the calming effect.

How It Helps:

- Grounds readers in the present moment, reducing the emotional overwhelm of the stressor.
- Provides a mental "reset" that can be used anytime, anywhere.

5. Journaling with E M D R Techniques

Journaling is a powerful tool for processing thoughts and emotions. By integrating E M D R principles, readers can enhance its effectiveness.

How to Practice E M D R-Inspired Journaling:

1. Write about a specific stressful situation, describing what happened and how it made you feel.
2. Identify the negative belief associated with the stressor (e.g., "I'm not good enough").
3. Create a positive belief to counter it (e.g., "I am learning and improving").
4. Engage in bilateral tapping while reading or reflecting on the positive belief.

Benefits:

- Encourages self-reflection and emotional clarity.
- Combines cognitive and physical processing to reduce stress and reinforce positive thinking.

6. Managing Future-Oriented Anxiety

Worrying about the unknown, such as upcoming deadlines or financial pressures, is a common source of stress. E M D R-inspired techniques help reframe these fears.

Steps to Handle Future Anxiety:

1. **Visualize Success**: Imagine yourself successfully navigating the situation you're worried about.
2. **Focus on Positive Beliefs**: Anchor thoughts like "I can adapt and handle this" with bilateral stimulation.
3. **Break It Down**: Use tapping while breaking the situation into manageable steps, reducing the sense of being overwhelmed.

Example: A reader worried about an upcoming job interview can visualize themselves answering questions confidently while engaging in BLS.

7. Calming the Nervous System with Bilateral Breathing

Combining breathing exercises with bilateral stimulation helps readers calm their body and mind during stressful moments.

How to Practice Bilateral Breathing:

1. Sit comfortably with your hands on your knees.
2. Tap alternately on your knees while inhaling deeply for four counts, holding for four, and exhaling for six.
3. Repeat for 1–2 minutes, focusing on the rhythm of your breath and the tapping.

Benefits:

- Quickly reduces physical symptoms of stress, such as a racing heart or shallow breathing.
- Enhances focus and clarity, making it easier to tackle the stressor.

8. Using the Butterfly Hug for Immediate Relief

The Butterfly Hug is a simple, self-soothing technique designed to provide immediate emotional regulation.

Steps to Practice the Butterfly Hug:

1. Cross your arms over your chest, placing your hands on opposite shoulders.
2. Gently tap your shoulders alternately, mimicking the flapping of butterfly wings.
3. Focus on a calming thought, such as "I am safe" or "This will pass."

When to Use It:

- During stressful meetings or phone calls.
- When feeling overwhelmed by daily tasks or responsibilities.

9. Handling Minor Conflicts

Arguments or misunderstandings can create lingering tension. E M D R-inspired techniques can help reprocess these experiences.

How to Handle a Conflict:

1. Identify the memory of the argument and how it made you feel.
2. Use BLS to process the emotions tied to the memory.
3. Replace thoughts like "I always mess up" with "I can communicate effectively and resolve conflicts."

Example: After a disagreement with a friend, a reader can use tapping while focusing on their belief, "I value my relationships and can make things right."

10. Building Resilience Through Regular Practice

Readers will learn how to incorporate these E M D R-inspired techniques into their daily routine to build long-term resilience.

How to Build a Practice:

- Start with 5–10 minutes of bilateral stimulation daily, focusing on positive beliefs or safe place visualization.
- Use tapping or breathing exercises as needed during stressful moments.
- Reflect on progress weekly, noting how responses to stressors improve over time.

What Readers Will Gain

By learning these E M D R-inspired techniques, readers will:

- Gain practical tools to manage daily stressors and anxiety.
- Develop greater emotional awareness and self-regulation skills.
- Reframe negative thoughts and beliefs into empowering, positive ones.
- Build resilience to navigate future challenges with confidence and calm.

Why It Stands Out: Practical Tips to Incorporate E M D R into Daily Routines with Mindfulness-Based Adaptations

This book stands out because it provides actionable, E M D R-inspired techniques seamlessly integrated into daily life. By combining E M D R principles with mindfulness practices, readers gain tools to enhance emotional regulation, reduce stress, and build resilience—all while maintaining their busy schedules. These adaptations make the transformative benefits of E M D R accessible beyond therapy sessions, empowering readers to use them proactively for mental well-being.

The Value of E M D R in Daily Routines

- **Accessibility**: Readers can practice these techniques anytime, anywhere—at home, during commutes, or at work.
- **Consistency**: Regular use of E M D R-inspired exercises builds emotional resilience over time.
- **Mind-Body Connection**: Pairing E M D R with mindfulness enhances self-awareness and fosters a deeper sense of calm and presence.

1. Morning Rituals: Setting a Positive Tone for the Day

Incorporating E M D R techniques into a morning routine helps ground the mind and body, preparing readers for a day of focus and clarity.

Practical Tip: Morning Bilateral Breathing

1. **Start with Breathing**: Sit comfortably and take slow, deep breaths.
2. **Add Bilateral Stimulation (BLS)**: While breathing, alternately tap your knees, shoulders, or thighs.
3. **Visualize a Positive Day**: Imagine yourself navigating your day with confidence and ease. Focus on positive affirmations, such as "I am capable and ready for today."

How It Helps:

- Promotes a calm, focused mindset.
- Reinforces positive beliefs, reducing anticipatory anxiety.

2. Mindful Movement: Enhancing Physical Activity with E M D R

Combining E M D R principles with physical activities like walking, yoga, or stretching brings mindfulness to movement and fosters emotional balance.

Practical Tip: Mindful Walking with BLS

1. Take a walk at a steady pace.
2. Focus on the alternating movement of your feet, noticing the sensation of each foot touching the ground.

3. Pair this with a calming affirmation, such as "With every step, I feel more grounded."

How It Helps:

- Grounds the mind in the present moment.
- Engages the brain's natural bilateral processing through physical movement.

3. Work Breaks: Managing Stress During the Day

Work-related stress can accumulate, impacting focus and productivity. Incorporating short, E M D R-inspired practices into breaks helps reset the mind and reduce tension.

Practical Tip: Butterfly Hug for Stress Relief

1. Cross your arms over your chest and place your hands on opposite shoulders.
2. Gently tap your shoulders alternately while taking slow, deep breaths.
3. Focus on a calming thought or affirmation, such as "I am calm and can handle this."

How It Helps:

- Quickly reduces stress and anxiety.
- Provides a discreet, effective way to regulate emotions in the workplace.

4. Transitioning from Work to Home: Letting Go of the Day

The transition between work and home life can be a source of stress. E M D R-inspired techniques help shift focus and create a sense of separation.

Practical Tip: Bilateral Journaling to Unwind

1. Write about any lingering thoughts or emotions from the day.
2. Identify one positive takeaway or accomplishment to focus on.
3. Engage in bilateral tapping (e.g., tapping your knees) as you reflect on the positive takeaway.

How It Helps:

- Releases negative energy and stress from the day.
- Reinforces positive reflections, creating a sense of closure.

5. Mindfulness-Based Adaptations for Emotional Regulation

Mindfulness practices, such as meditation and grounding exercises, align perfectly with E M D R principles. Readers can integrate these adaptations to enhance their mindfulness routines.

Practical Tip: Safe Place Meditation

1. Find a quiet space and sit comfortably.
2. Close your eyes and visualize a "safe place" where you feel calm and secure (e.g., a beach, forest, or favorite room).
3. While holding this image, gently tap alternately on your knees or shoulders.
4. Focus on the sights, sounds, and sensations of your safe place, allowing yourself to fully immerse in the experience.

How It Helps:

- Grounds the mind and body in a calming, positive state.

- Provides an emotional anchor to return to during moments of stress.

6. Evening Wind-Down: Preparing for Restful Sleep

Incorporating E M D R techniques into an evening routine helps process lingering stress and quiet the mind for better sleep.

Practical Tip: Bedtime Visualization with BLS

1. Lie down in bed and close your eyes.
2. Reflect on one positive moment from the day, no matter how small.
3. Use bilateral tapping, such as gently tapping your thighs or shoulders alternately, while focusing on the positive memory.
4. Pair this with slow, deep breathing to relax your body.

How It Helps:

- Promotes a sense of gratitude and peace.
- Reduces anxious thoughts, facilitating restful sleep.

7. Dealing with Stress in Real Time

When unexpected stressors arise during the day, quick E M D R-inspired practices can help readers regain control and clarity.

Practical Tip: Bilateral Grounding on the Go

1. Sit or stand in a quiet space.
2. Begin tapping alternately on your knees or thighs.
3. Focus on the physical sensations around you (e.g., the feel of the ground under your feet, the temperature of the air).

4. Repeat a calming affirmation, such as "I am present and can handle this."

How It Helps:

- Quickly calms the nervous system in moments of stress.
- Redirects focus from the stressor to the present moment.

8. Regular Self-Reflection: Building Resilience Over Time

Incorporating regular self-reflection enhances the effectiveness of E M D R-inspired techniques, allowing readers to track progress and adjust their routines.

Practical Tip: Weekly Reflection with E M D R Principles

1. Set aside 10 minutes at the end of each week.
2. Write about a situation where you successfully managed stress.
3. Reflect on the positive beliefs or coping mechanisms you used.
4. Engage in bilateral tapping while visualizing future challenges and how you will handle them with confidence.

How It Helps:

- Reinforces positive coping mechanisms.
- Builds resilience by linking past successes to future challenges.

Why These Tips Work

- **Science-Backed**: These practices leverage E M D R's proven ability to regulate emotions and reframe beliefs.
- **Time-Efficient**: They integrate into existing routines, making them easy to adopt and sustain.
- **Mindfulness-Enhanced**: Combining E M D R with mindfulness practices deepens emotional awareness and promotes long-term well-being.

Chapter 8: Healing Emotional Wounds in Relationships

Relationships, whether romantic, familial, or platonic, can bring immense joy, but they can also be a source of deep emotional pain. Unresolved conflicts, breaches of trust, or unmet expectations can leave lasting emotional wounds, often creating barriers to intimacy and understanding. E M D R (Eye Movement Desensitization and Reprocessing) therapy offers a powerful framework for addressing these wounds, helping individuals and partners process past hurts, improve communication, and rebuild trust.

This chapter explores how E M D R principles can be applied to heal emotional wounds in relationships, offering practical strategies for fostering healthier and more connected bonds.

Understanding Emotional Wounds in Relationships

Emotional wounds often arise from:

- **Miscommunication**: Misunderstandings or unspoken needs leading to feelings of neglect or rejection.
- **Betrayal**: Breaches of trust, such as infidelity or dishonesty, that erode the foundation of a relationship.
- **Unresolved Conflicts**: Recurring arguments that remain unaddressed, creating resentment over time.
- **Past Trauma**: Individual histories of trauma that affect how partners perceive and respond to each other.

These wounds, if left unhealed, can manifest as:

- Difficulty trusting others.
- Emotional distancing or avoidance.
- Intense reactions to minor conflicts.

- Patterns of blame or self-doubt.

1. Identifying Emotional Wounds

The first step to healing is recognizing and understanding the emotional wounds affecting the relationship.

Practical Exercise: Mapping Emotional Wounds

1. **Reflect**: Take time to think about specific incidents that caused hurt in the relationship.
2. **Journal**: Write about the emotions tied to these incidents—anger, sadness, fear, or guilt.
3. **Identify Beliefs**: Note any negative beliefs formed as a result, such as "I can't trust anyone" or "I'm not worthy of love."

Why It Helps:

- Encourages self-awareness and clarity about the root causes of tension in the relationship.
- Provides a foundation for constructive conversations and healing.

2. Healing Personal Wounds with E M D R Techniques

Before addressing relationship issues collectively, individuals can work on their own emotional triggers and past experiences that contribute to conflict.

Practical Tip: Safe Place Visualization

1. Create a mental "safe place" where you feel secure and calm.
2. Use bilateral tapping while visualizing this place to reinforce a sense of emotional safety.
3. Practice this exercise before difficult conversations to enter them with a clear and calm mindset.

Reprocessing Past Experiences

1. Identify a memory of a past argument or betrayal that still feels emotionally charged.
2. Focus on the memory while engaging in bilateral stimulation, such as tapping on your knees or shoulders.
3. Replace negative beliefs like "I always mess things up" with positive ones like "I am learning to communicate effectively."

Why It Helps:

- Reduces the emotional intensity of past wounds, making it easier to approach current conflicts with understanding rather than defensiveness.

3. Rebuilding Trust in Relationships

Trust is a cornerstone of healthy relationships, and E M D R principles can help rebuild it by addressing the pain of betrayal or dishonesty.

Practical Tip: Reframing the Narrative

1. Identify the specific incident that caused a breach of trust.
2. Write down the negative belief it created, such as "I can't rely on my partner."
3. Reflect on evidence that challenges this belief (e.g., times when your partner has been supportive or honest).
4. Pair this reflection with bilateral tapping to integrate a more balanced perspective.

Collaborative Healing

- Partners can practice sharing how they felt during the breach of trust using "I" statements (e.g., "I felt hurt because I needed reassurance and didn't receive it").
- Engage in mutual grounding exercises, such as deep breathing or gentle tapping together, to create a sense of emotional connection and safety.

Why It Helps:

- Reframing the narrative allows individuals to see the relationship more holistically rather than fixating on a single incident.
- Collaborative practices foster empathy and rebuild emotional intimacy.

4. Improving Communication Through E M D R Techniques

Poor communication often perpetuates emotional wounds in relationships. E M D R-inspired exercises can enhance clarity, reduce emotional reactivity, and promote active listening.

Practical Tip: Emotional Check-Ins

1. Set aside 10–15 minutes daily to share feelings and experiences with your partner.
2. Use bilateral stimulation (e.g., holding hands and tapping alternately) during the conversation to reduce tension and promote emotional openness.
3. Focus on expressing needs and feelings without blame, using statements like "I feel [emotion] because I need [need]."

Managing Arguments

1. Pause during heated moments to engage in self-soothing techniques, such as the Butterfly Hug.
2. Reflect on what triggered your reaction and whether it ties to unresolved past experiences.
3. Revisit the conversation with a calm and solution-focused mindset.

Why It Helps:

- Reduces the likelihood of miscommunication by fostering a calm, attentive state.
- Creates a habit of addressing conflicts constructively rather than reactively.

5. Healing Shared Trauma

In some relationships, partners may have experienced shared trauma, such as a loss, accident, or significant life challenge. E M D R can help process these experiences collectively.

Practical Tip: Joint Visualization Exercise

1. Sit together in a quiet space and close your eyes.
2. Visualize a moment of mutual support or joy in your relationship.
3. Use bilateral tapping (e.g., tapping each other's hands alternately) while focusing on this positive memory.
4. Share your reflections with each other to reinforce the bond.

Why It Helps:

- Shifts the focus from the trauma to the strength and resilience of the partnership.
- Enhances emotional connection by creating a shared sense of positivity.

6. Building Resilience for the Future

Healing emotional wounds is not just about addressing the past—it's about building the tools to navigate future challenges together.

Practical Tip: Weekly Relationship Check-Ins

1. Schedule a time each week to discuss the state of your relationship.
2. Begin with a grounding exercise, such as bilateral breathing or the Butterfly Hug, to enter the conversation calmly.
3. Use a simple framework:
   - **What went well this week?**
   - **What challenges arose?**
   - **What can we do better moving forward?**

Creating Emotional Safety Plans

- Develop a plan for handling conflicts, including agreed-upon timeouts and grounding techniques.
- Commit to practicing E M D R-inspired exercises individually and as a couple during moments of stress.

Why It Helps:

- Prevents unresolved issues from escalating by fostering regular, open communication.
- Strengthens the relationship's foundation by prioritizing emotional safety and mutual growth.

Real-Life Success Story

Case Study: Sarah and James

- **The Challenge**: Sarah and James struggled with recurring arguments stemming from a breach of trust during James's career transition.

- **The Solution**: They incorporated E M D R-inspired practices into their routine, such as:
    - Individually reprocessing moments of frustration using tapping and safe place visualization.
    - Practicing daily emotional check-ins with bilateral stimulation to foster empathy.
    - Using joint visualization exercises to reinforce their commitment to mutual support.
- **The Outcome**: Over time, Sarah and James rebuilt trust and improved communication, creating a healthier, more connected relationship.

What Readers Will Learn: How E M D R Can Repair Emotional Wounds from Breakups, Betrayal, or Difficult Family Dynamics

Readers will discover how **Eye Movement Desensitization and Reprocessing (E M D R)** can address the deep emotional wounds caused by breakups, betrayal, and strained family relationships. These types of emotional pain often leave lingering feelings of rejection, mistrust, or unresolved anger, which can significantly impact mental well-being and future relationships. Through E M D R's structured framework, readers can reprocess painful memories, challenge negative beliefs, and build healthier perspectives, enabling healing and emotional freedom.

1. Repairing Emotional Wounds from Breakups

Breakups often leave behind a tangle of unresolved emotions—sadness, anger, guilt, or even feelings of failure. E M D R can help individuals process the end of a relationship and move forward with clarity and self-compassion.

How E M D R Helps with Breakups

- **Reprocessing Painful Memories**: E M D R targets moments tied to the breakup, such as the last argument or feelings of abandonment, reducing their emotional charge.

- **Challenging Negative Beliefs**: Breakups can trigger harmful thoughts like "I'm unlovable" or "I'll never find happiness again." E M D R helps replace these beliefs with affirmations like "I deserve love and fulfillment."
- **Letting Go of Regret**: Through bilateral stimulation, E M D R aids in releasing guilt or "what-if" scenarios, fostering acceptance and peace.

Example: Sarah's Story

Scenario: Sarah, a 32-year-old teacher, felt stuck after her partner ended their three-year relationship, believing she wasn't good enough.

E M D R Solution:

- **Target Memory**: The moment her partner told her it was over.
- **Negative Belief**: "I am not worthy of love."
- **Positive Belief**: "I am deserving of love and respect."
- **Outcome**: After several E M D R sessions, Sarah found relief from the weight of rejection and started approaching new relationships with confidence.

2. Healing from Betrayal

Betrayal, whether from a partner, friend, or family member, can shatter trust and leave individuals feeling emotionally unsafe. E M D R helps rebuild trust in others and fosters self-reliance.

How E M D R Helps with Betrayal

- **Processing the Incident**: E M D R revisits the betrayal, such as discovering a partner's infidelity or a friend's dishonesty, to reprocess its emotional impact.

- **Rebuilding Trust**: The therapy replaces beliefs like "I can't trust anyone" with "I can choose who to trust based on their actions."
- **Reducing Hypervigilance**: E M D R calms the heightened fear of future betrayal, enabling healthier boundaries and relationships.

Example: James's Story

Scenario: James, a 40-year-old entrepreneur, struggled to trust his new partner after his previous relationship ended due to infidelity.
E M D R Solution:

- **Target Memory**: The day he discovered his ex-partner's betrayal.
- **Negative Belief**: "I'll always be betrayed."
- **Positive Belief**: "I can set boundaries and trust wisely."
- **Outcome**: E M D R helped James let go of the fear of repeated betrayal, allowing him to build a healthy connection with his new partner.

3. Addressing Difficult Family Dynamics

Family dynamics can be a source of lifelong emotional pain. Parental neglect, sibling rivalry, or toxic relationships often leave individuals feeling stuck in patterns of anger, guilt, or inadequacy.

How E M D R Helps with Family Dynamics

- **Breaking Negative Cycles**: E M D R targets formative family experiences that shaped limiting beliefs, such as "I'll never be good enough" or "I have to earn love."
- **Processing Triggers**: Family interactions often evoke strong emotional reactions tied to past wounds.

E M D R helps desensitize these triggers, enabling more neutral responses.
- **Fostering Self-Compassion**: E M D R encourages individuals to separate their worth from family expectations or criticisms.

Example: Maria's Story

Scenario: Maria, a 28-year-old artist, felt constant pressure to meet her parents' high expectations, leading to anxiety and self-doubt.

E M D R Solution:

- **Target Memory**: A childhood memory of being told she wasn't trying hard enough.
- **Negative Belief**: "I'm a failure."
- **Positive Belief**: "I am valuable regardless of others' opinions."
- **Outcome**: E M D R helped Maria detach from her parents' critical voice, building self-worth and confidence in her career.

4. Letting Go of Resentment

Resentment often builds in the aftermath of unresolved conflicts in relationships. E M D R can help release this emotional burden, paving the way for forgiveness or acceptance.

How E M D R Helps with Resentment

- **Reprocessing Anger**: E M D R desensitizes memories of hurtful incidents, allowing individuals to process anger constructively.
- **Shifting Perspectives**: The therapy reframes the conflict, helping individuals focus on growth rather than blame.

- **Fostering Closure**: E M D R supports letting go of resentment without requiring reconciliation, prioritizing the individual's emotional peace.

Example: Lisa's Story

Scenario: Lisa, a 35-year-old manager, couldn't let go of anger toward her sibling after a heated argument about family finances.
E M D R Solution:

- **Target Memory**: The argument that escalated the resentment.
- **Negative Belief**: "I can't forgive them."
- **Positive Belief**: "I can move forward and set boundaries."
- **Outcome**: E M D R helped Lisa release the emotional weight of the conflict, enabling her to reestablish a healthier relationship with her sibling.

5. E M D R for Rebuilding Relationships

For those looking to repair relationships, E M D R can address the underlying emotional wounds that hinder reconciliation.

Steps for Rebuilding Relationships with E M D R Principles

1. **Identify Core Issues**: Focus on the incidents that created emotional distance or mistrust.
2. **Reprocess Emotional Pain**: Use bilateral stimulation to reduce the emotional intensity tied to these memories.
3. **Reframe Beliefs**: Replace thoughts like "They don't care about me" with "We can rebuild trust through communication."
4. **Practice Mutual Grounding**: Engage in shared grounding exercises, such as deep breathing or

visualization, to foster connection during difficult conversations.

What Readers Will Gain

Through this chapter, readers will:

- Understand how E M D R can target specific relational wounds, whether from breakups, betrayal, or family dynamics.
- Learn how to process painful memories and triggers tied to relational conflicts.
- Replace limiting beliefs with empowering affirmations that support healing and growth.
- Gain practical tools for fostering trust, releasing resentment, and approaching relationships with a renewed sense of clarity and confidence.

Why It Stands Out: Focuses on Healing Interpersonal Trauma and Includes Exercises for Couples or Family Members

This book stands out because it uniquely addresses **interpersonal trauma**, recognizing the profound impact that relational wounds—caused by betrayals, conflicts, or unmet emotional needs—can have on individuals, couples, and families. It goes beyond individual healing by offering **practical exercises designed for shared participation**, enabling partners and family members to navigate emotional pain together, rebuild trust, and strengthen bonds. By integrating **E M D R-inspired techniques** into these relational dynamics, the book provides a transformative approach to fostering empathy, connection, and mutual healing.

Why Interpersonal Trauma Matters

Interpersonal trauma, stemming from betrayal, abandonment, or repeated conflicts, often leaves individuals:

- Struggling with trust and intimacy.
- Feeling emotionally unsafe or disconnected in relationships.
- Reacting defensively or avoiding vulnerability with loved ones.

This type of trauma can perpetuate cycles of pain within relationships unless addressed directly. E M D R's ability to target and reprocess relational triggers makes it an ideal framework for healing interpersonal wounds, whether between partners, parents and children, or siblings.

1. Exercises for Couples: Rebuilding Trust and Connection

When trauma impacts a relationship, it often creates barriers to communication and trust. These exercises help couples process emotional pain together, fostering understanding and rebuilding emotional safety.

Exercise 1: Joint Safe Place Visualization

1. **Purpose**: Create a shared sense of calm and emotional safety.
2. **Steps**:
   - Sit together in a quiet space.
   - Each partner closes their eyes and imagines a "safe place" that feels calming and secure.
   - Share your visualizations with each other, describing the details of your safe place (e.g., "I see a beach with soft waves").
   - Hold hands or tap each other's hands alternately while focusing on the shared feeling of safety.
3. **Why It Helps**:
   - Promotes vulnerability and emotional openness.
   - Establishes a mutual sense of security to return to during conflicts or emotional triggers.

Exercise 2: Reprocessing Relationship Triggers

1. **Purpose**: Address recurring arguments or misunderstandings by reframing their emotional roots.
2. **Steps**:
   - Identify a specific argument or conflict that caused hurt (e.g., a disagreement about finances or parenting styles).
   - Each partner takes turns sharing how the incident made them feel, using "I" statements (e.g., "I felt unheard when...").
   - Engage in bilateral stimulation (such as tapping knees alternately) while focusing on the memory of the conflict.
   - Replace negative beliefs about the relationship (e.g., "We'll never get past this") with positive beliefs (e.g., "We can work through challenges together").
3. **Why It Helps**:
   - Reduces the emotional intensity tied to the memory of the conflict.
   - Encourages empathy by allowing each partner to understand the other's perspective.

2. Exercises for Families: Healing Collective Trauma

Families often carry unresolved conflicts or patterns of dysfunction that affect their emotional well-being. These exercises provide tools for processing shared pain and fostering connection.

Exercise 1: Family Emotional Check-In

1. **Purpose**: Create a space for family members to share feelings and build emotional awareness.
2. **Steps**:

- Set aside 15–20 minutes weekly for an open discussion.
- Each family member shares one positive experience from the week and one challenge they faced.
- Use a grounding technique, such as bilateral tapping, during the discussion to maintain calm and focus.
- Conclude by setting a shared goal for the week (e.g., "Let's practice listening to each other without interrupting").

3. **Why It Helps**:
- Encourages open communication and mutual support.
- Helps family members feel heard and validated.

Exercise 2: Reprocessing Shared Trauma

1. **Purpose**: Address collective experiences that have caused stress or pain (e.g., the loss of a loved one, financial hardship, or a shared accident).
2. **Steps**:
- Gather as a family in a comfortable space.
- Identify the shared trauma and allow each member to express their feelings about it.
- Engage in a family-wide bilateral stimulation exercise, such as holding hands and gently squeezing alternately while focusing on a comforting thought or memory.
- Discuss one way the family has grown stronger despite the trauma.
3. **Why It Helps**:
- Reduces the emotional intensity of the shared experience.
- Reinforces the family's resilience and ability to overcome challenges together.

3. Exercises for Parents and Children: Repairing Bonds

Parent-child relationships often carry emotional wounds from unmet expectations, misunderstandings, or repeated conflicts. These exercises help repair and strengthen the bond.

Exercise 1: Parent-Child Visualization

1. **Purpose**: Reconnect emotionally through shared mindfulness.
2. **Steps**:
   - Sit together in a quiet space, facing each other.
   - The parent guides the child through a calming visualization (e.g., "Imagine we're walking in a sunny garden").
   - Use bilateral stimulation, such as gently tapping the child's shoulders, while describing the scene.
   - Conclude by sharing one thing you appreciate about each other.
3. **Why It Helps**:
   - Builds trust and emotional closeness.
   - Helps the child feel seen and valued.

Exercise 2: Repairing After a Conflict

1. **Purpose**: Address lingering tension after an argument or misunderstanding.
2. **Steps**:
   - Each person identifies how the conflict made them feel (e.g., "I felt frustrated because I wasn't understood").
   - Use bilateral tapping while reflecting on the incident to reduce its emotional intensity.
   - Share one thing you learned from the conflict and one step to avoid similar situations in the future.

3. **Why It Helps**:
   - Teaches emotional regulation and accountability.
   - Encourages healthy conflict resolution skills.

4. Why E M D R Works for Interpersonal Trauma

- **Targets Emotional Roots**: E M D R goes beyond surface-level conflicts to address the memories, triggers, and beliefs that fuel relational pain.
- **Promotes Mutual Healing**: By including exercises for partners or families, E M D R fosters shared understanding and collective growth.
- **Builds Resilience**: Regular use of E M D R-inspired techniques strengthens communication and emotional awareness, reducing the likelihood of future conflicts.

What Readers Will Gain

Through this focus on interpersonal trauma, readers will:

- Learn how to address emotional wounds caused by betrayal, conflict, or neglect in relationships.
- Gain tools to process and reframe painful memories with loved ones.
- Foster healthier communication patterns and rebuild trust with partners or family members.
- Strengthen their ability to navigate relational challenges with empathy and resilience.

Chapter 9: Overcoming Obstacles During E M D R Therapy

While Eye Movement Desensitization and Reprocessing (E M D R) therapy is a powerful tool for healing trauma, anxiety, and emotional wounds, it's not uncommon to encounter challenges during the therapeutic process. These obstacles can range from difficulty accessing memories to feeling overwhelmed by emotions. Understanding these hurdles and learning how to navigate them effectively is crucial for making progress and achieving long-term healing.

This chapter provides an in-depth exploration of common obstacles faced during E M D R therapy and offers practical strategies for overcoming them, ensuring that readers can maximize the benefits of their therapeutic journey.

1. Understanding Common Obstacles in E M D R Therapy

E M D R therapy involves processing deeply rooted emotions and beliefs, which can sometimes lead to challenges such as:

- **Blocked Memories**: Difficulty recalling or accessing specific events or emotions.
- **Overwhelm**: Feeling emotionally flooded during reprocessing.
- **Resistance**: Hesitation to confront painful memories or fear of change.
- **Negative Cognitions**: Persistent beliefs that feel resistant to reframing.
- **Physical Sensations**: Discomfort or tension in the body during sessions.

Each of these obstacles is a natural part of the healing process and can be addressed with appropriate strategies and support.

2. Overcoming Blocked Memories

Blocked memories are often a defense mechanism used by the brain to protect against overwhelming emotions. While this can be frustrating during E M D R therapy, there are ways to gently access these memories.

Strategies for Accessing Blocked Memories:

- **Safe Place Visualization**: Start with a calming visualization exercise to create a sense of safety and openness.
- **Focus on Sensations**: If memories feel out of reach, focus on physical sensations, emotions, or vague impressions tied to the event. These can act as breadcrumbs leading to the memory.
- **Timeline Exercise**: Construct a timeline of your life, marking significant events. This can help jog memories without forcing recall.
- **Stay Patient**: Trust that the memory will surface when you are emotionally ready to process it.

3. Managing Emotional Overwhelm

Feeling overwhelmed during E M D R sessions is a common experience, especially when processing traumatic or highly charged memories. It's important to have tools in place to regulate emotions.

Strategies for Managing Overwhelm:

- **Grounding Techniques**:
    - Focus on your breath, inhaling deeply and exhaling slowly.
    - Use bilateral tapping (e.g., tapping knees alternately) to bring attention back to the present.
- **Use a Safe Place Anchor**:

- Pause the session to visualize your safe place, reinforcing feelings of security.
- **Pace Yourself**:
    - Let your therapist know if the session feels too intense. Slowing down or revisiting less distressing memories first can help build emotional resilience.
- **Develop Coping Tools**:
    - Practice calming techniques outside of therapy, such as meditation or progressive muscle relaxation, to increase your emotional bandwidth.

4. Addressing Resistance

Resistance in E M D R therapy often stems from fear of confronting painful emotions or uncertainty about change. Acknowledging and understanding this resistance is the first step toward overcoming it.

Strategies for Addressing Resistance:

- **Explore the Fear**:
    - Ask yourself what feels most intimidating about the process. Are you afraid of the emotions that might surface, or are you unsure of what life will look like without the weight of your trauma?
- **Set Small Goals**:
    - Break the therapy process into manageable steps, focusing on small wins rather than the entire journey.
- **Reaffirm Your Motivation**:
    - Reflect on why you started therapy and the life you hope to build after healing.
- **Collaborate with Your Therapist**:
    - Share your concerns openly. Your therapist can adjust the pace or focus to help you feel more comfortable.

5. Working Through Persistent Negative Beliefs

One of E M D R's primary goals is to reframe negative beliefs into positive, empowering ones. However, some beliefs may feel deeply ingrained or resistant to change.

Strategies for Reframing Negative Beliefs:

- **Focus on Evidence**:
    - Challenge negative beliefs by identifying evidence that contradicts them. For example, if you believe "I am not capable," reflect on times when you succeeded despite challenges.
- **Pair Positive Beliefs with BLS**:
    - Use bilateral stimulation (e.g., tapping or eye movements) while focusing on a positive affirmation, reinforcing its emotional impact.
- **Start Small**:
    - If "I am worthy of love" feels too ambitious, start with "I am learning to value myself" and gradually build toward stronger affirmations.
- **Revisit Earlier Phases**:
    - Sometimes persistent beliefs require further work on earlier memories. Revisiting foundational experiences can provide clarity and create space for change.

6. Coping with Physical Sensations

Trauma is often stored in the body, and E M D R sessions may bring up physical sensations such as tightness, tingling, or discomfort. These sensations are a normal part of processing and can be managed with mindfulness.

Strategies for Managing Physical Sensations:

- **Body Awareness**:
    - Notice where you feel tension or discomfort without judgment. Label the sensation (e.g.,

"tightness in my chest") to bring awareness without overwhelm.
  - **Grounding Through Movement**:
    - Incorporate gentle movement, such as stretching or shaking out your hands, to release stored energy.
- **Pair with Breathing**:
    - Combine deep breathing with BLS to soothe the body and mind simultaneously.
- **Discuss with Your Therapist**:
    - Share these sensations during your session. Your therapist can adjust the approach or suggest additional coping strategies.

7. Navigating Plateaus in Progress

It's not uncommon to feel stuck or as though progress has slowed during E M D R therapy. Plateaus are a normal part of the healing process and often indicate a need for reflection or adjustment.

Strategies for Breaking Through Plateaus:

- **Reassess Goals**:
    - Reflect on your initial therapy goals and whether they need adjustment based on your progress so far.
- **Celebrate Small Wins**:
    - Recognize even minor changes, such as reduced emotional intensity or improved sleep, as signs of progress.
- **Try New Techniques**:
    - Explore alternative methods within E M D R, such as using different bilateral stimulation techniques or revisiting earlier memories.
- **Take Breaks**:
    - Sometimes stepping back and focusing on self-care can recharge your emotional capacity for deeper work.

8. Strengthening Support Systems

Healing through E M D R can be emotionally taxing, making it essential to have a strong support system in place.

Strategies for Building Support:

- **Share Your Journey**:
    - Talk to trusted friends or family members about your therapy process, helping them understand your experiences.
- **Seek Peer Support**:
    - Join support groups or forums where others share their E M D R journeys, fostering connection and encouragement.
- **Prioritize Self-Care**:
    - Engage in activities that replenish your energy, such as exercise, creative hobbies, or spending time in nature.

9. Preparing for Post-E M D R Growth

As therapy progresses, it's important to prepare for the changes and growth that come with healing. This includes learning how to integrate insights gained during E M D R into daily life.

Strategies for Post-E M D R Integration:

- **Reflect Regularly**:
    - Journaling about your experiences and progress helps solidify new beliefs and emotional patterns.
- **Practice Coping Tools**:
    - Continue using grounding exercises and BLS techniques during moments of stress.
- **Embrace New Perspectives**:

- Be open to exploring new relationships, activities, or opportunities that align with your healed self.

What Readers Will Gain

By addressing common obstacles in E M D R therapy, readers will:

- Gain confidence in navigating challenges during their healing journey.
- Develop tools for managing emotional overwhelm, resistance, and physical sensations.
- Learn how to reframe persistent negative beliefs and overcome progress plateaus.
- Strengthen their resilience and readiness for long-term emotional growth.

What Readers Will Learn: Common Challenges and Setbacks in E M D R Therapy, and How to Work Through Them

E M D R (Eye Movement Desensitization and Reprocessing) therapy is a powerful tool for addressing trauma, anxiety, and emotional wounds. However, like any healing journey, it comes with its challenges and setbacks. These obstacles can arise from the complexity of the therapy, the intensity of emotions, or the deeply rooted nature of certain memories and beliefs. This section will equip readers with an understanding of these challenges and provide actionable strategies to navigate them effectively, ensuring progress and emotional growth.

1. Common Challenges in E M D R Therapy
Challenge 1: Difficulty Accessing Memories

Some individuals struggle to recall specific memories or details during E M D R sessions. This can happen due to:

- **Blocked memories** caused by trauma-related dissociation.
- A lack of clarity about the origins of certain emotions or triggers.
- The brain's natural defense mechanisms to avoid revisiting painful experiences.

How to Work Through It:

- **Focus on Emotions or Sensations**: Instead of trying to remember exact details, concentrate on the feelings or physical sensations tied to the issue. E M D R can work effectively even without a clear memory.
- **Use Imagery or Hypotheticals**: If memories feel inaccessible, use a related image or scenario that evokes similar emotions as a starting point.
- **Be Patient**: Trust that your mind will reveal what it's ready to process. Working with less distressing memories first can help build trust and unlock deeper recollections over time.

Challenge 2: Feeling Overwhelmed by Emotions

Processing trauma can bring up intense emotions, such as fear, sadness, or anger, which may feel overwhelming during or after a session.

How to Work Through It:

- **Grounding Techniques**:
    - Use **bilateral stimulation (BLS)**, such as tapping or following a moving object, to center yourself.
    - Engage in deep breathing exercises, inhaling for four counts, holding for four, and exhaling for six.
- **Pause and Reflect**: It's okay to pause a session if emotions become too intense. Discuss this with your therapist to slow the pace of processing.

- **Practice Emotional Regulation Outside Sessions**: Techniques like mindfulness, progressive muscle relaxation, or journaling can help increase your tolerance for emotional intensity.

Challenge 3: Resistance to the Process

Some individuals feel hesitant to engage fully in E M D R due to:

- Fear of confronting painful memories.
- Uncertainty about what life will look like after healing.
- Skepticism about the effectiveness of the therapy.

How to Work Through It:

- **Identify the Root of Resistance**:
  - Reflect on what feels most intimidating about the process. Are you worried about reliving the pain, or are you unsure of your ability to handle it?
- **Start Small**:
  - Begin with less distressing memories or emotions to build confidence in the process.
- **Reaffirm Your Goals**:
  - Remind yourself why you started E M D R. Focus on the long-term benefits of healing and the life you want to create.
- **Communicate with Your Therapist**:
  - Share your concerns openly. A supportive therapist can adjust the pace or method to help you feel more comfortable.

Challenge 4: Persistent Negative Beliefs

Certain negative beliefs, such as "I'm not good enough" or "I'll never be safe," can feel deeply ingrained and resistant to change.

How to Work Through It:

- **Identify Evidence Against the Belief**:
  - Reflect on times in your life that contradict the negative belief. For example, if you believe "I can't succeed," think of moments when you overcame challenges.
- **Use Positive Affirmations Gradually**:
  - If a positive belief like "I am worthy" feels too ambitious, start with something more approachable, such as "I am learning to value myself."
- **Revisit Foundational Memories**:
  - Sometimes, deeply rooted beliefs require processing earlier or more significant memories. Revisiting these can unlock insights and create space for change.

Challenge 5: Physical Discomfort

Trauma is often stored in the body, and E M D R sessions may bring up physical sensations, such as tightness, heaviness, or restlessness.

How to Work Through It:

- **Acknowledge the Sensations**:
  - Pay attention to where the discomfort is located in your body and describe it without judgment (e.g., "I feel tightness in my chest").
- **Incorporate Movement**:
  - Gentle movements, such as stretching or shaking out your hands, can help release physical tension.
- **Pair with Breathing**:
  - Use deep breathing exercises to calm your nervous system and alleviate physical symptoms.
- **Discuss with Your Therapist**:

- Share these sensations during sessions. Your therapist may adjust the approach or offer additional coping tools.

Challenge 6: Progress Plateaus

It's normal to feel stuck or experience a plateau during E M D R therapy. This can happen when progress slows or emotional intensity doesn't decrease as expected.

How to Work Through It:

- **Reassess Your Goals**:
  - Reflect on your initial therapy goals and whether they need adjustment. Progress may be happening in subtle ways, such as improved sleep or reduced irritability.
- **Celebrate Small Wins**:
  - Acknowledge even minor improvements, such as being less triggered by certain situations or feeling more hopeful.
- **Explore Alternative Techniques**:
  - Discuss trying new BLS methods, such as auditory or tactile stimulation, to refresh the process.
- **Take Breaks**:
  - Sometimes, stepping back from deep processing and focusing on self-care can recharge your emotional capacity.

Challenge 7: Post-Session Distress

It's not uncommon to feel emotionally vulnerable or experience heightened sensitivity after an E M D R session, as your brain continues to process memories and emotions.

How to Work Through It:

- **Plan for Recovery:**

- Schedule some quiet time after sessions to reflect and recharge. Avoid overloading your schedule immediately after therapy.
- **Engage in Soothing Activities**:
  - Practice grounding techniques, spend time in nature, or engage in hobbies that bring comfort.
- **Keep a Journal**:
  - Writing about post-session emotions can help you track progress and identify patterns in your healing journey.
- **Stay in Communication**:
  - Let your therapist know about any post-session distress. They can provide guidance and adjust future sessions as needed.

What Readers Will Gain

By understanding these common challenges and setbacks, readers will:

1. Recognize that obstacles are a natural part of the healing process, not a sign of failure.
2. Develop effective strategies to navigate difficulties, such as emotional overwhelm, resistance, or physical discomfort.
3. Feel empowered to communicate openly with their therapist and take an active role in their healing.
4. Gain confidence in their ability to overcome setbacks and continue progressing toward emotional freedom and resilience.

Why It Stands Out: Practical Advice to Help Readers Troubleshoot Issues Like Emotional Overwhelm or Therapy Resistance

This book stands out because it provides **clear, actionable strategies** to address common challenges that may arise during E M D R therapy. Emotional overwhelm and therapy resistance are two of the most frequent obstacles in the healing process. Instead of allowing these difficulties to hinder progress, readers will learn how to identify, understand, and work through these issues effectively. The book equips readers with tools to manage intense emotions, build resilience, and address internal hesitations, empowering them to stay engaged and achieve lasting healing.

1. Addressing Emotional Overwhelm

Emotional overwhelm occurs when the intensity of emotions during E M D R therapy feels too much to process. This can leave individuals feeling stuck or hesitant to continue their sessions. Instead of avoiding these emotions, this book helps readers take control of their emotional experiences.

Key Signs of Emotional Overwhelm:

- Feeling emotionally flooded during or after a session.
- Experiencing persistent distressing thoughts or memories.
- Avoiding therapy sessions due to fear of emotional intensity.

Practical Strategies to Manage Emotional Overwhelm:

- **Grounding Techniques**:
    - Use simple grounding exercises like focusing on your breath, naming five things you see around you, or placing your hands under running water to anchor yourself in the present moment.
- **Safe Place Visualization**:
    - Pause the session and return to a mental "safe place" to calm your mind and body. Visualize every detail of this safe place, such as the sights, sounds, and smells, while engaging in bilateral tapping.

- **Scale Down Emotional Intensity**:
    - Work with your therapist to process less distressing memories first, gradually building up your emotional resilience for deeper issues.
- **Post-Session Care Plan**:
    - Schedule time after therapy for self-care activities, such as journaling, walking in nature, or practicing yoga, to help regulate emotions.

Why It Works: These strategies help reduce the intensity of emotions, allowing readers to stay engaged with therapy while feeling emotionally safe and in control.

2. Navigating Therapy Resistance

Resistance can manifest as avoidance, skepticism, or hesitancy to engage fully with the therapeutic process. This is often a defense mechanism rooted in fear—fear of confronting painful emotions, fear of failure, or even fear of change.

Key Signs of Therapy Resistance:

- Canceling or rescheduling sessions frequently.
- Feeling stuck or uninterested in exploring certain memories.
- Believing that therapy isn't working or doubting the process.

Practical Strategies to Overcome Resistance:

- **Identify the Source of Resistance**:
    - Reflect on what makes you hesitant. Are you afraid of reliving the trauma? Worried about emotional discomfort? Pinpointing the cause of resistance is the first step toward addressing it.
- **Set Small, Achievable Goals**:

- Break down therapy into manageable steps. Focus on one memory or belief at a time, celebrating small wins along the way.
- **Reframe Therapy as Growth**:
  - Instead of seeing therapy as reliving the past, view it as an opportunity to free yourself from the grip of old patterns and beliefs.
- **Communicate with Your Therapist**:
  - Share your concerns openly. A supportive therapist can adjust the pace, use grounding techniques, or offer reassurance to help you feel more comfortable.
- **Anchor Yourself in Motivation**:
  - Write down why you started therapy and what you hope to achieve. Reflect on this during moments of resistance to reignite your commitment.

Why It Works: These strategies transform resistance from a roadblock into a learning opportunity, helping readers reframe their fears and remain engaged in the healing process.

3. Managing the Fear of Emotional Intensity

For many, the anticipation of emotional intensity can be just as daunting as the emotions themselves. This fear often leads to avoidance or hesitation, making it harder to progress in therapy.

Practical Advice to Address Fear:

- **Practice Pre-Session Visualization**:
  - Before a session, visualize yourself calmly and confidently engaging in therapy. Imagine a successful session where you feel empowered, even in the face of difficult emotions.
- **Build Emotional "Safety Nets"**:

- Prepare grounding tools, such as a favorite calming object, music, or a safe word with your therapist, to help you feel secure during intense moments.
- **Focus on Progress, Not Perfection**:
  - Remind yourself that therapy is a process, not a performance. Even small steps forward are significant.
- **Embrace the Present Moment**:
  - Use mindfulness techniques, such as focusing on your breath or the physical sensations in your body, to stay grounded in the present rather than fearing what might arise.

Why It Works: By proactively addressing the fear of emotional intensity, readers can reduce avoidance behaviors and approach therapy with greater confidence.

4. Building Resilience for Long-Term Success

Healing through E M D R therapy is not linear; setbacks and emotional challenges are a natural part of the process. This book helps readers build resilience, ensuring that they stay the course even when difficulties arise.

Practical Strategies to Build Resilience:

- **Develop a Support Network**:
  - Share your journey with trusted friends, family, or support groups who can offer encouragement and validation.
- **Track Your Progress**:
  - Keep a journal to document changes, such as improved sleep, reduced triggers, or a sense of emotional balance. Recognizing progress, no matter how small, reinforces motivation.
- **Practice Self-Compassion**:
  - Treat yourself with kindness during challenging moments. Remind yourself that

healing takes time and that every step forward
is meaningful.
- **Incorporate Daily E M D R Tools**:
  - Use E M D R-inspired techniques, such as
    bilateral tapping or safe place visualization,
    outside of therapy sessions to maintain
    emotional stability.

Why It Works: These strategies create a solid foundation
for readers to manage challenges, celebrate progress, and
remain committed to their healing journey.

5. Turning Setbacks into Opportunities

Setbacks in therapy, such as feeling stuck or experiencing
heightened emotions, can feel discouraging. This book
redefines setbacks as opportunities for growth and self-
discovery.

Practical Steps to Reframe Setbacks:

- **Reflect on the Experience**:
  - Ask yourself: What triggered this setback?
    What can I learn from it? Use setbacks as a way
    to better understand your emotional patterns.
- **Discuss with Your Therapist**:
  - Bring up challenges during your sessions. Your
    therapist can offer new perspectives or
    techniques to address these obstacles.
- **Celebrate the Effort**:
  - Acknowledge the courage it takes to face
    emotional pain, even when progress feels slow.

Why It Works: By viewing setbacks as a normal part of
healing, readers can maintain a sense of hope and resilience
throughout their E M D R journey.

Chapter 10: Integrating E M D R with Other Therapies

While E M D R (Eye Movement Desensitization and Reprocessing) therapy is highly effective for addressing trauma, anxiety, and emotional challenges, its benefits can be amplified when combined with other therapeutic approaches. Integrating E M D R with complementary therapies, such as Cognitive Behavioral Therapy (CBT), mindfulness, or somatic therapies, allows for a more comprehensive healing process. This chapter explores how E M D R can work synergistically with other modalities to enhance emotional resilience, address complex issues, and promote holistic well-being.

1. Why Integrate E M D R with Other Therapies?

No single therapeutic approach addresses every facet of emotional healing. By integrating E M D R with other evidence-based methods, individuals can:

- **Target Different Layers of Healing**: E M D R focuses on reprocessing traumatic memories, while other therapies address cognitive patterns, body awareness, or interpersonal dynamics.
- **Provide Versatility**: Combining approaches allows therapy to be tailored to the individual's unique needs and goals.
- **Reinforce Progress**: Techniques from complementary therapies can solidify and sustain the gains made during E M D R sessions.

2. Integrating E M D R with Cognitive Behavioral Therapy (CBT)

CBT is an effective therapy for identifying and challenging negative thought patterns and beliefs. When paired with E M

D R, CBT can help address cognitive distortions while E M D R focuses on the emotional and somatic aspects of trauma.

How It Works Together:

- **CBT Identifies Negative Beliefs**:
    - CBT techniques help pinpoint maladaptive thoughts, such as "I am powerless" or "I'll never be happy."
- **E M D R Reprocesses the Root Causes**:
    - E M D R addresses the traumatic memories or events that created these beliefs.
- **CBT Reinforces Positive Beliefs**:
    - Post-E M D R, CBT techniques (e.g., thought tracking and behavioral experiments) help solidify new, empowering beliefs.

Example Integration:

- During CBT, a client identifies a belief like "I am not good enough" and learns how it affects their behavior.
- In E M D R, the client processes the early memory that planted this belief, reducing its emotional charge.
- After E M D R, CBT tools help the client challenge any residual doubts and build confidence through actionable steps.

3. Integrating E M D R with Mindfulness Practices

Mindfulness, which emphasizes present-moment awareness and nonjudgmental acceptance, complements E M D R by helping individuals regulate emotions and build resilience.

How It Works Together:

- **Mindfulness Prepares for E M D R**:

- Mindfulness exercises, such as deep breathing or body scans, help clients feel grounded and emotionally stable before sessions.
- **Mindfulness Supports Processing**:
  - During E M D R, mindfulness encourages individuals to observe emotions and memories without judgment, fostering smoother reprocessing.
- **Mindfulness Enhances Post-Session Integration**:
  - After E M D R, mindfulness practices reinforce the client's ability to stay present and manage stress effectively.

Example Integration:

- Before an E M D R session, the therapist guides the client through a mindfulness exercise to reduce anxiety.
- During reprocessing, the client uses mindful awareness to notice emotions and sensations as they arise.
- Between sessions, the client practices mindfulness daily to maintain emotional balance and reduce triggers.

4. Integrating E M D R with Somatic Therapies

Somatic therapies focus on the connection between the mind and body, addressing how trauma is stored physically. E M D R's bilateral stimulation and somatic techniques work synergistically to release tension and promote healing.

How It Works Together:

- **Somatic Awareness Enhances E M D R:**
  - Techniques like tracking body sensations or breathwork deepen the client's connection to

their physical experiences during E M D R sessions.

- **E M D R Aids Somatic Release**:
  - By reprocessing traumatic memories, E M D R helps release physical tension or discomfort tied to those experiences.
- **Somatic Techniques Aid Regulation**:
  - Between E M D R sessions, somatic exercises like gentle stretching or grounding movements help clients manage stress and stay present.

Example Integration:

- A client with trauma-related chest tightness uses somatic therapy to become aware of the sensation.
- During E M D R, the client reprocesses a memory that triggered this tension, leading to its gradual release.
- After the session, the client practices somatic grounding exercises to reinforce the sense of calm.

5. Integrating E M D R with Dialectical Behavior Therapy (DBT)

DBT is particularly effective for individuals who struggle with intense emotions or interpersonal difficulties. Its emphasis on emotional regulation and coping skills complements E M D R's focus on trauma resolution.

How It Works Together:

- **DBT Prepares for E M D R**:
  - DBT skills, such as distress tolerance and emotion regulation, help clients manage intense emotions during E M D R.
- **E M D R Resolves Core Traumas**:
  - E M D R addresses the traumatic events that underlie emotional dysregulation.
- **DBT Sustains Progress**:

- After E M D R, DBT techniques support ongoing emotional balance and healthy relationships.

Example Integration:

- A client uses DBT's "STOP" skill (Stop, Take a step back, Observe, Proceed) to ground themselves during a challenging E M D R session.
- After E M D R reprocessing, the client practices DBT's interpersonal effectiveness skills to improve communication and set boundaries in relationships.

6. Integrating E M D R with Narrative Therapy

Narrative therapy helps clients reframe their personal stories, shifting from a problem-focused perspective to one of empowerment. When paired with E M D R, it enables individuals to rewrite their narratives with reduced emotional pain.

How It Works Together:

- **Narrative Therapy Identifies Themes**:
  - Clients explore how their life stories have been shaped by trauma and identify disempowering patterns.
- **E M D R Reprocesses Key Events**:
  - E M D R reduces the emotional charge of specific memories tied to these narratives.
- **Narrative Therapy Reframes the Story**:
  - After E M D R, clients rewrite their stories, focusing on growth, resilience, and empowerment.

Example Integration:

- A client who views themselves as a victim explores this theme in narrative therapy.

- During E M D R, they process a memory that reinforced this belief, reducing its emotional grip.
- Post-E M D R, they rewrite their story with a focus on their strength and survival.

7. Integrating E M D R with Art Therapy

Art therapy uses creative expression to explore emotions and experiences, offering a non-verbal outlet for healing. Combined with E M D R, it provides additional ways to access and process trauma.

How It Works Together:

- **Art Therapy Uncovers Themes**:
    - Clients use drawing, painting, or other creative mediums to express emotions or memories, identifying targets for E M D R.
- **E M D R Processes Emotional Content**:
    - Bilateral stimulation helps reprocess the emotions and themes expressed through art.
- **Art Therapy Enhances Integration**:
    - After E M D R sessions, art therapy helps clients explore and solidify insights gained during reprocessing.

Example Integration:

- A client creates a drawing representing a painful childhood memory.
- In E M D R, they focus on this memory, reducing its emotional intensity.
- Post-session, the client uses art to express their evolving feelings of empowerment and healing.

8. The Benefits of a Holistic Approach

Integrating E M D R with other therapies creates a well-rounded approach to healing by addressing the mind, body, and emotions. This synergy provides:

- **Comprehensive Healing**: Multiple modalities tackle the emotional, cognitive, and physical impacts of trauma.
- **Adaptability**: Techniques can be tailored to the client's preferences and progress.
- **Sustainability**: Complementary therapies offer ongoing tools for self-care and growth beyond E M D R sessions.

What Readers Will Learn: How E M D R Complements Other Therapies Like CBT, Mindfulness, and Talk Therapy

Readers will discover how **Eye Movement Desensitization and Reprocessing (E M D R)** can work hand-in-hand with other therapeutic approaches, such as Cognitive Behavioral Therapy (CBT), mindfulness practices, and traditional talk therapy. Each of these modalities offers unique strengths, and integrating them with E M D R allows for a more comprehensive and effective healing process. By understanding how these therapies complement each other, readers will learn how to create a personalized and synergistic approach to addressing trauma, anxiety, and emotional challenges.

1. Complementing Cognitive Behavioral Therapy (CBT)

CBT focuses on identifying and changing negative thought patterns and beliefs that influence behavior and emotions. While CBT works on a cognitive level, E M D R complements it by addressing the emotional and somatic roots of these beliefs, often stemming from unresolved trauma.

How They Work Together:

- **CBT Pinpoints Negative Beliefs**:
  - CBT helps individuals identify harmful thought patterns, such as "I am not good enough" or "I'll never succeed."
- **E M D R Reprocesses Underlying Memories**:
  - E M D R targets the memories or experiences that created these beliefs, reducing their emotional intensity and impact.
- **CBT Reinforces New Beliefs**:
  - After E M D R sessions, CBT tools, such as thought tracking and behavioral experiments, help solidify positive beliefs and support long-term behavioral changes.

Example:

- A client with social anxiety identifies the thought, "People will judge me," during CBT sessions.
- In E M D R, the client reprocesses a childhood memory of being ridiculed by classmates, reducing its emotional charge.
- Post-E M D R, CBT techniques help the client build confidence by practicing positive affirmations like "I can connect with people."

What Readers Will Learn: How E M D R addresses the emotional core of negative beliefs while CBT provides tools to reshape thought patterns and behaviors.

2. Complementing Mindfulness Practices

Mindfulness, which emphasizes present-moment awareness and nonjudgmental acceptance, enhances E M D R's effectiveness by fostering emotional regulation and self-awareness. Similarly, E M D R deepens the benefits of mindfulness by addressing unresolved emotional triggers that disrupt present-moment focus.

How They Work Together:

- **Mindfulness Prepares for E M D R:**
  - Mindfulness practices, such as breathing exercises or body scans, help clients enter E M D R sessions with a calm and focused mindset.
- **E M D R Resolves Disruptive Triggers:**
  - By reprocessing traumatic memories, E M D R reduces the intensity of emotions that interrupt mindfulness practices, such as intrusive thoughts or flashbacks.
- **Mindfulness Sustains Healing:**
  - Post-E M D R, mindfulness techniques help individuals maintain emotional balance and stay grounded in the present.

Example:

- A client with P T S D practices mindfulness meditation but struggles with intrusive thoughts about a traumatic event.
- E M D R sessions help reprocess the traumatic memory, reducing its emotional grip and allowing the client to deepen their meditation practice.
- The client continues using mindfulness as a tool for emotional regulation and stress management.

What Readers Will Learn: How mindfulness enhances E M D R by promoting calm and awareness, while E M D R reduces emotional barriers to mindfulness.

3. Complementing Talk Therapy

Traditional talk therapy provides a safe space for individuals to explore their emotions, experiences, and relationships. While talk therapy focuses on understanding and verbalizing issues, E M D R complements it by directly addressing unresolved emotional pain stored in the mind and body.

How They Work Together:

- **Talk Therapy Explores Patterns**:
    - Clients gain insight into their thoughts, behaviors, and relationship dynamics through open discussions with their therapist.
- **E M D R Targets Specific Memories**:
    - E M D R reprocesses the painful memories that talk therapy uncovers, helping to resolve emotional triggers and reduce distress.
- **Talk Therapy Integrates E M D R Insights**:
    - After E M D R sessions, talk therapy helps individuals reflect on the changes in their emotional and cognitive patterns, fostering deeper self-awareness.

Example:

- A client explores a pattern of self-sabotage in relationships during talk therapy.
- Through E M D R, the client reprocesses a memory of rejection by a caregiver, which had shaped their fear of intimacy.
- Talk therapy helps the client integrate this healing into their relationships, exploring healthier ways to connect with others.

What Readers Will Learn: How E M D R provides emotional resolution while talk therapy offers the framework to explore and integrate these changes.

4. Enhancing Emotional Regulation

One of E M D R's strengths is its ability to regulate intense emotions during reprocessing. This can be further supported by tools from other therapies to help individuals manage distress during and after sessions.

Key Techniques:

- **From Mindfulness**:
    - Techniques like deep breathing and body scans help clients stay grounded when emotions become overwhelming during E M D R.
- **From CBT**:
    - Tools like cognitive restructuring help challenge and replace unhelpful thoughts that arise during or after reprocessing.
- **From Talk Therapy**:
    - Reflective discussions provide emotional validation and help clients contextualize their experiences.

What Readers Will Learn: How to combine tools from multiple therapies to maintain emotional stability and progress.

5. Building Resilience Through Integration

Integrating E M D R with other therapies helps build long-term resilience by addressing both the roots of emotional pain and the skills needed to navigate life's challenges.

Holistic Benefits:

- **Emotional Healing**:
    - E M D R resolves trauma and reduces emotional intensity, creating space for growth.
- **Cognitive Flexibility**:
    - CBT fosters adaptive thinking patterns and behaviors, supporting resilience.
- **Present-Moment Awareness**:
    - Mindfulness enhances self-regulation and reduces stress.
- **Relational Growth**:
    - Talk therapy improves interpersonal dynamics and communication skills.

Example:

- A client dealing with workplace anxiety uses mindfulness to stay present during meetings.
- E M D R helps resolve a memory of public embarrassment that contributes to their anxiety.
- CBT tools, like thought tracking, help them challenge negative beliefs about their performance.
- Talk therapy explores ways to improve communication with colleagues and supervisors.

What Readers Will Learn: How combining E M D R with other therapies provides a multi-layered approach to emotional growth and resilience.

6. Practical Tips for Integrating E M D R with Other Therapies

Readers will learn actionable steps to create a personalized therapeutic approach:

- **Communicate Goals with Your Therapist**:
  - Share your interest in combining E M D R with other modalities to ensure a cohesive treatment plan.
- **Use Techniques Between Sessions**:
  - Practice mindfulness exercises or CBT tools between E M D R sessions to reinforce progress.
- **Track Progress Across Modalities**:
  - Keep a journal to reflect on how each therapy complements the other and contributes to your healing.
- **Be Open to Experimentation**:
  - Explore different combinations of therapies to find what works best for your unique needs.

What Readers Will Gain

Through this section, readers will:

- Understand how E M D R complements therapies like CBT, mindfulness, and talk therapy by addressing trauma from multiple angles.
- Learn how each therapy's strengths—cognitive restructuring, emotional regulation, and relational exploration—enhance E M D R's impact.
- Discover practical strategies for integrating E M D R with other modalities to create a personalized and effective healing process.
- Gain confidence in navigating their therapeutic journey with a comprehensive toolkit for emotional growth and resilience.

Why It Stands Out: Readers Learn to Create a Holistic Recovery Plan, Leveraging Multiple Therapeutic Modalities

This book distinguishes itself by empowering readers to develop a **holistic recovery plan** that integrates multiple therapeutic modalities, including E M D R, Cognitive Behavioral Therapy (CBT), mindfulness, talk therapy, and somatic practices. Healing from trauma, anxiety, or emotional pain is rarely one-dimensional. By combining the unique strengths of different approaches, readers can address the root causes of distress, enhance emotional resilience, and sustain long-term well-being.

Through practical guidance and actionable strategies, readers will learn to craft a personalized plan that addresses their unique needs and goals, making the healing process both effective and transformative.

1. The Value of a Holistic Recovery Plan

A holistic recovery plan recognizes that healing involves the mind, body, and emotions. It goes beyond addressing symptoms to focus on long-term growth and resilience.

Key Benefits:

- **Comprehensive Healing**: By combining multiple therapies, readers can tackle emotional pain from different angles—cognitive, emotional, and physical.
- **Personalization**: A multi-modality approach allows readers to tailor their recovery plan to their specific needs, challenges, and preferences.
- **Sustainability**: Integrating ongoing practices like mindfulness or somatic exercises ensures that healing continues beyond therapy sessions.

2. Integrating E M D R as the Core of the Recovery Plan

E M D R serves as the foundation for the holistic recovery plan by addressing the root causes of emotional pain—traumatic memories and negative beliefs. Its structured eight-phase approach ensures that readers process distressing events while building emotional resilience.

How E M D R Fits Into a Holistic Plan:

- **Root-Cause Healing**: E M D R focuses on resolving the traumatic memories that drive emotional distress, paving the way for deeper recovery.
- **Emotional Regulation**: Techniques like bilateral stimulation help readers manage emotional overwhelm during and after therapy.
- **Complementary Role**: E M D R works seamlessly alongside other modalities, enhancing their effectiveness by addressing unresolved emotional triggers.

3. Leveraging Cognitive Behavioral Therapy (CBT)

CBT complements E M D R by equipping readers with tools to challenge and replace negative thought patterns. While E

M D R addresses the emotional and somatic roots of trauma, CBT provides cognitive strategies to sustain progress.

How CBT Enhances Recovery:

- Identifying harmful thoughts and beliefs that contribute to anxiety or depression.
- Teaching practical coping strategies, such as reframing and thought tracking.
- Reinforcing the positive beliefs and insights gained during E M D R sessions.

Example: A reader reprocesses a childhood memory of rejection through E M D R and uses CBT techniques to challenge ongoing thoughts like "I'm not good enough," replacing them with affirmations like "I am capable and valuable."

4. Incorporating Mindfulness Practices

Mindfulness, with its emphasis on present-moment awareness and emotional regulation, plays a vital role in maintaining balance throughout the recovery process. It complements E M D R by helping readers stay grounded and reduce stress.

How Mindfulness Fits Into the Plan:

- **Before E M D R**: Mindfulness exercises, such as deep breathing or body scans, prepare readers for therapy by calming the nervous system.
- **During Integration**: After E M D R sessions, mindfulness helps readers reflect on and solidify emotional insights.
- **For Daily Life**: Ongoing mindfulness practices enhance resilience, reduce anxiety, and improve emotional awareness.

Example: A reader uses mindfulness to navigate heightened emotions between E M D R sessions, focusing on grounding techniques like noticing their breath or engaging in a mindful walk.

5. Including Somatic Therapy for Body Awareness

Trauma often manifests physically, with lingering tension or discomfort stored in the body. Somatic therapy works alongside E M D R to release these physical symptoms and promote holistic healing.

How Somatic Therapy Complements E M D R:

- **Body Awareness**: Helps readers identify where trauma is stored in the body, such as tightness in the chest or shoulders.
- **Tension Release**: Combines gentle movements, such as stretching or shaking, to release built-up tension after E M D R sessions.
- **Grounding**: Incorporates body-focused exercises, such as progressive muscle relaxation, to help readers manage stress and stay present.

Example: After reprocessing a traumatic memory with E M D R, a reader practices somatic exercises like grounding through their feet to release residual tension and feel more connected to the present.

6. Using Talk Therapy for Reflection and Integration

Traditional talk therapy provides a space for readers to explore their emotions, relationships, and personal growth in depth. It serves as a valuable complement to E M D R's memory-focused approach.

How Talk Therapy Enhances Recovery:

- **Emotional Exploration**: Helps readers discuss and process the changes they experience during E M D R.
- **Relationship Building**: Offers insights into how trauma affects interpersonal dynamics, fostering healthier communication and boundaries.
- **Integration Support**: Guides readers in applying the lessons learned from E M D R to their daily lives.

Example: A reader uses talk therapy to reflect on how reprocessing a traumatic memory in E M D R has shifted their perspective on a current relationship.

7. Sustaining Progress with Self-Care Practices

A holistic recovery plan includes self-care practices that reinforce the therapeutic work done in E M D R and other modalities. These practices ensure that healing continues between sessions and beyond.

Key Self-Care Practices:

- **Journaling**: Helps readers track emotional patterns, insights, and progress over time.
- **Exercise**: Regular physical activity reduces stress and boosts mood, supporting emotional balance.
- **Creative Expression**: Art, music, or writing provides an outlet for processing emotions and fostering self-discovery.
- **Nature Connection**: Spending time outdoors promotes relaxation and a sense of grounding.

Example: A reader incorporates journaling to reflect on their E M D R sessions and uses exercise to manage post-session stress.

8. Practical Steps to Create a Holistic Recovery Plan

Readers will learn actionable steps to develop their personalized recovery plan:

1. **Identify Goals**: Define what they hope to achieve through therapy, such as reducing anxiety, improving relationships, or resolving trauma.
2. **Choose Modalities**: Work with a therapist to select the best combination of E M D R, CBT, mindfulness, talk therapy, or somatic practices.
3. **Establish a Routine**: Integrate therapeutic practices, such as mindfulness or journaling, into daily life for ongoing support.
4. **Monitor Progress**: Regularly assess emotional, cognitive, and physical improvements, adjusting the plan as needed.

What Readers Will Gain

Through this chapter, readers will:

- Understand the benefits of integrating multiple therapeutic modalities with E M D R.
- Learn how to create a recovery plan that addresses their unique needs and challenges.
- Gain tools for managing emotional, cognitive, and physical aspects of healing.
- Build a sustainable framework for long-term emotional growth and resilience.

Chapter 11: Real-Life Success Stories

Nothing illustrates the transformative power of E M D R therapy more vividly than real-life success stories. These accounts provide hope and inspiration, showing readers that healing from trauma, anxiety, and emotional wounds is possible. Each story highlights a unique challenge, the process of navigating E M D R therapy, and the outcomes that changed lives. By sharing these stories, this chapter offers encouragement and relatable experiences that readers can draw strength from on their own healing journey.

1. Sarah: Overcoming Childhood Neglect

Background:

Sarah, a 32-year-old teacher, grew up in a home where her emotional needs were neglected. Her parents, overwhelmed by financial stress, rarely showed affection or praised her achievements. As an adult, Sarah struggled with low self-esteem, people-pleasing tendencies, and fear of abandonment in relationships.

The E M D R Journey:

- **Target Memory**: Sarah reprocessed memories of being ignored by her parents when she sought their attention as a child.
- **Negative Belief**: "I'm not important."
- **Positive Belief**: "I matter, and my needs are valid."
- **Therapeutic Process**: Through E M D R, Sarah revisited specific incidents, such as being dismissed when asking for help with homework, and gradually reduced their emotional charge.

Outcome:

After several sessions, Sarah experienced a profound shift in her self-perception. She began asserting her needs in relationships and recognized her inherent worth, independent of others' approval. Her newfound confidence allowed her to pursue leadership roles at work and form healthier, more balanced connections.

2. James: Healing Combat P T S D
Background:

James, a 38-year-old combat veteran, returned home after multiple deployments with severe P T S D. He experienced flashbacks, hypervigilance, and emotional numbness, which strained his relationship with his family and left him feeling disconnected from civilian life.

The E M D R Journey:

- **Target Memory**: James focused on a traumatic ambush during his deployment, where he lost two comrades.
- **Negative Belief**: "I failed to protect my team."
- **Positive Belief**: "I did everything I could."
- **Therapeutic Process**: E M D R helped James reprocess the vivid imagery and survivor's guilt tied to the ambush. Bilateral stimulation allowed him to reframe the event, recognizing his bravery and dedication during an impossible situation.

Outcome:

James experienced fewer flashbacks and found himself able to engage in daily activities without constant fear. His emotional connection with his wife and children improved, and he began volunteering to support other veterans, channeling his experiences into a meaningful purpose.

3. Priya: Letting Go of Social Anxiety
Background:

Priya, a 27-year-old marketing professional, avoided social interactions due to severe anxiety. Her fear of being judged or embarrassing herself kept her from speaking up in meetings or attending networking events, limiting her career growth.

The E M D R Journey:

- **Target Memory**: Priya reprocessed a childhood memory of being laughed at during a class presentation.
- **Negative Belief**: "I'm not good at speaking."
- **Positive Belief**: "I can express myself clearly and confidently."
- **Therapeutic Process**: E M D R helped Priya reframe the memory of humiliation and replace the fear associated with public speaking with feelings of calm and control.

Outcome:

Priya's confidence grew as she began participating more actively at work and building professional relationships. She delivered her first major presentation with poise and even started mentoring junior colleagues, something she never thought she could do.

4. Maria: Rebuilding After Betrayal
Background:

Maria, a 40-year-old entrepreneur, discovered her partner of 10 years had been unfaithful. The betrayal left her feeling broken, questioning her self-worth, and doubting her ability to trust again.

The E M D R Journey:

- **Target Memory**: Maria reprocessed the moment she found evidence of the betrayal.
- **Negative Belief**: "I'm not enough."
- **Positive Belief**: "I am worthy of love and respect."
- **Therapeutic Process**: Through E M D R, Maria addressed the emotional pain tied to the betrayal and the deeper wounds it had triggered from earlier experiences of rejection.

Outcome:

Maria reclaimed her sense of self-worth and independence. She set healthy boundaries in future relationships and no longer blamed herself for her partner's actions. E M D R gave her the strength to forgive—not for reconciliation, but to free herself from the burden of resentment.

5. David: Navigating Grief and Loss
Background:

David, a 50-year-old widower, struggled with unresolved grief after losing his wife to cancer. He avoided talking about her, fearing the intensity of his emotions, and found himself stuck in a cycle of guilt and sadness.

The E M D R Journey:

- **Target Memory**: David processed the day his wife passed and his belief that he could have done more to ease her suffering.
- **Negative Belief**: "I failed her."
- **Positive Belief**: "I loved her and did my best."
- **Therapeutic Process**: E M D R helped David revisit both painful and joyful memories, gradually reducing his guilt and allowing him to focus on the love they shared.

Outcome:

David found peace with his loss and began honoring his wife's memory by creating a scholarship in her name. He reconnected with his children, sharing stories about their mother and embracing life with a renewed sense of purpose.

6. Lisa: Breaking Free from Complex P T S D
Background:

Lisa, a 35-year-old graphic designer, endured years of emotional abuse from a controlling parent. She struggled with perfectionism, self-doubt, and recurring nightmares tied to her childhood experiences.

The E M D R Journey:

- **Target Memories**: Lisa worked through key incidents of verbal and emotional abuse, such as being criticized for her achievements.
- **Negative Belief**: "I'll never be good enough."
- **Positive Belief**: "I am enough, just as I am."
- **Therapeutic Process**: E M D R allowed Lisa to reprocess these memories incrementally, starting with less distressing events to build emotional resilience before tackling core experiences.

Outcome:

Lisa let go of the perfectionism that had dictated her life. She began celebrating her successes without seeking external validation and set firm boundaries with her parent, reclaiming her sense of self-worth.

7. Mark: Conquering Fear of Driving After an Accident

Background:

Mark, a 29-year-old accountant, avoided driving for two years after surviving a severe car accident. The thought of getting behind the wheel triggered panic attacks and flashbacks.

The E M D R Journey:

- **Target Memory**: Mark reprocessed the moment of impact and the fear he felt immediately afterward.
- **Negative Belief**: "I'm not safe."
- **Positive Belief**: "I can drive safely and confidently."
- **Therapeutic Process**: E M D R desensitized the traumatic memory and helped Mark replace fear with a sense of control.

Outcome:

Mark gradually returned to driving, starting with short trips and building up to longer commutes. He regained his independence and confidence, no longer feeling controlled by his past.

What Readers Will Learn

From these success stories, readers will:

- **Gain Hope and Inspiration**: See how others have navigated challenges similar to their own and emerged stronger.
- **Understand E M D R's Versatility**: Learn how E M D R can address a wide range of emotional wounds, from childhood trauma to grief, anxiety, and P T S D.
- **Visualize the Process**: Get a clear picture of how E M D R works in real-life scenarios, including the therapeutic journey and resulting transformations.

- **Feel Empowered**: Recognize that healing is possible, even for deeply rooted emotional pain.

What Readers Will Learn: Inspiring Accounts of Individuals Who've Healed Through E M D R

This chapter provides readers with **real-life accounts of individuals who have transformed their lives** through E M D R therapy. These stories highlight the profound ability of E M D R to address deep-seated trauma, anxiety, grief, and emotional pain. By sharing the challenges, breakthroughs, and victories of diverse individuals, readers will gain a deeper understanding of how E M D R works and what it can achieve. These accounts aim to inspire hope, reduce feelings of isolation, and empower readers to believe in their own capacity for healing.

1. Healing Childhood Trauma: Sarah's Journey to Self-Worth

Overview:

Sarah, a 34-year-old teacher, struggled with feelings of inadequacy rooted in her childhood. Growing up in a household where emotional neglect was common, Sarah internalized the belief that she was unworthy of love and attention.

How E M D R Helped:

- Sarah's therapy focused on processing memories of being ignored by her parents during key moments of her development, such as school events or when seeking comfort.
- Her **negative belief**, "I am unimportant," was replaced with the **positive belief**, "I am valuable and deserving of love."
- Through bilateral stimulation, Sarah desensitized the emotional pain tied to these memories, reducing their hold on her present life.

Outcome:

Sarah became more confident in her personal and professional relationships. She began advocating for herself at work, resulting in a promotion, and developed healthier boundaries with her family.

Key Takeaway: Readers will learn how E M D R can help reframe limiting beliefs formed in childhood, leading to newfound confidence and self-worth.

2. Reclaiming Life After Trauma: James's Story of Overcoming P T S D

Overview:

James, a combat veteran, returned from deployment with severe P T S D. He experienced frequent flashbacks, insomnia, and an inability to engage in daily activities without feeling hypervigilant.

How E M D R Helped:

- James reprocessed the memory of a traumatic ambush that led to the loss of two comrades. This memory carried intense guilt and self-blame.
- E M D R allowed him to see the event from a more compassionate perspective, shifting his belief from "I failed them" to "I did my best in an impossible situation."
- The therapy also addressed triggers, such as loud noises, which previously caused panic.

Outcome:

James began sleeping peacefully for the first time in years. He reconnected with his family, started attending community events, and became a mentor for other veterans facing similar challenges.

Key Takeaway: Readers will understand how E M D R can provide relief from the debilitating symptoms of P T S D, helping individuals regain control over their lives.

3. Letting Go of Anxiety: Priya's Path to Confidence

Overview:

Priya, a marketing professional in her late 20s, struggled with debilitating social anxiety. The thought of public speaking or attending networking events left her paralyzed with fear.

How E M D R Helped:

- Priya's therapy targeted a childhood memory of being laughed at during a school presentation, which had cemented the belief, "I can't do anything right."
- Through E M D R, she desensitized the emotional charge of this memory and replaced it with the belief, "I can express myself clearly and confidently."
- Her therapist introduced visualization techniques during bilateral stimulation, where Priya imagined herself successfully navigating professional scenarios.

Outcome:

Priya delivered her first presentation at work with confidence, earning praise from her colleagues. She began attending networking events, building valuable professional relationships, and even mentoring junior team members.

Key Takeaway: Readers will see how E M D R can help address specific anxieties, unlocking personal and professional growth.

4. Healing Grief: David's Journey Through Loss
Overview:

David, a 50-year-old father, struggled to move forward after the sudden loss of his wife. He avoided discussing her, fearing the intensity of his emotions, and felt stuck in a cycle of guilt and sadness.

How E M D R Helped:

- E M D R sessions focused on the day his wife passed and his belief that he hadn't done enough to comfort her.
- Through bilateral stimulation, David reprocessed this memory, reframing his belief from "I failed her" to "I loved her and did my best."
- The therapy also helped David recall positive memories of their life together, reducing the dominance of his grief.

Outcome:

David began to honor his wife's memory by sharing stories about her with his children and starting a community support group for widowers. He felt a renewed sense of purpose and peace.

Key Takeaway: Readers will learn how E M D R can help reframe grief and guilt, transforming loss into an opportunity for healing and connection.

5. Breaking Free from Complex P T S D: Lisa's Transformation
Overview:

Lisa, a 35-year-old graphic designer, endured years of emotional abuse from a controlling parent. She battled perfectionism, self-doubt, and recurring nightmares tied to her childhood experiences.

How E M D R Helped:

- Lisa worked on key memories of verbal abuse, such as being told she wasn't good enough or smart enough.
- Her **negative belief**, "I will always fail," was replaced with the empowering thought, "I am capable and resilient."
- E M D R sessions also addressed her physical symptoms, such as tightness in her chest and frequent headaches, which gradually diminished.

Outcome:

Lisa let go of the unrealistic standards she set for herself and started celebrating her achievements. She established healthy boundaries with her parent and began to thrive personally and professionally.

Key Takeaway: Readers will see how E M D R can address deeply ingrained patterns of self-doubt, allowing individuals to reclaim their confidence and independence.

6. Overcoming Fear: Mark's Recovery After a Car Accident

Overview:

Mark, a 29-year-old accountant, avoided driving after a traumatic car accident. The thought of getting behind the wheel triggered panic attacks and flashbacks.

How E M D R Helped:

- Mark's therapy targeted the memory of the accident, particularly the moment of impact.

- E M D R reduced the intensity of his fear by reframing his belief, "I'm not safe," into "I can drive safely and confidently."
- The therapy also used gradual exposure, combining visualization techniques with bilateral stimulation to help Mark imagine himself driving calmly.

Outcome:

Mark started with short drives around his neighborhood and eventually returned to his daily commute. He regained his independence and no longer felt defined by his fear.

Key Takeaway: Readers will learn how E M D R can address specific phobias and fears, restoring a sense of safety and control.

7. Restoring Trust: Maria's Healing from Betrayal

Overview:

Maria, a 40-year-old entrepreneur, was devastated after discovering her partner of 10 years had been unfaithful. The betrayal left her questioning her self-worth and ability to trust others.

How E M D R Helped:

- E M D R focused on the memory of uncovering the betrayal, reducing the emotional pain tied to it.
- Maria reprocessed her belief, "I'm not enough," and replaced it with "I am worthy of love and respect."
- Therapy also addressed earlier memories of rejection that had compounded her feelings of unworthiness.

Outcome:

Maria rebuilt her self-esteem and developed healthier boundaries in future relationships. She forgave—not for reconciliation, but to free herself from the burden of anger and resentment.

Key Takeaway: Readers will see how E M D R can help individuals move past betrayal, rebuilding trust in themselves and others.

What Readers Will Gain

Through these inspiring accounts, readers will:

- **Understand the Power of E M D R**: See how it addresses diverse emotional wounds, from childhood trauma to grief and P T S D.
- **Find Relatable Stories**: Connect with the challenges and breakthroughs of others who have faced similar struggles.
- **Build Hope**: Recognize that healing and transformation are possible, no matter how deep the pain.
- **Gain Clarity**: Learn how E M D R works in real-life scenarios, including the step-by-step process and its lasting impact.

Why It Stands Out: Diverse, Relatable Success Stories Motivate Readers and Provide Hope

This book stands out because it includes a wide range of **diverse and relatable success stories**, illustrating how E M D R therapy has transformed the lives of individuals from all walks of life. These stories not only validate the struggles of readers who may feel alone in their pain but also offer **hope and inspiration** by showcasing tangible examples of healing and resilience. By highlighting the varied ways E M D R can address different challenges—from P T S D and anxiety to grief and relationship struggles—this book empowers readers to believe in their own capacity for recovery.

1. Representation of Diverse Experiences

The success stories in this book reflect the vast range of issues that E M D R can address, offering relatable examples for readers with different backgrounds, traumas, and emotional struggles.

What Readers Will Find:

- **Trauma Survivors**: Stories of individuals overcoming childhood neglect, combat-related P T S D, or physical abuse.
- **Anxiety and Phobia Management**: Accounts of people conquering social anxiety, fear of driving, or public speaking challenges.
- **Healing Relationships**: Experiences of those rebuilding trust after betrayal, navigating family conflict, or recovering from breakups.
- **Grief Recovery**: Narratives of individuals processing the loss of loved ones and finding peace.
- **Everyday Challenges**: Success stories of overcoming workplace stress, perfectionism, and self-doubt.

Why It Stands Out: The diversity of stories ensures that every reader can see a part of themselves in the journey of others, fostering a sense of connection and shared humanity.

2. Real-Life Transformation in Tangible Steps

Each story provides a **step-by-step account of the healing process**, helping readers understand how E M D R therapy works in practical terms. This detailed breakdown demystifies the therapy, making it approachable and less intimidating.

What Readers Will Learn:

- The emotional and physical symptoms individuals faced before therapy.
- Specific memories or triggers targeted during E M D R sessions.
- The shift in negative beliefs (e.g., "I'm powerless" to "I am in control").
- The tools and techniques used, such as bilateral stimulation, grounding exercises, or visualizations.
- The positive outcomes and long-term changes experienced.

Why It Stands Out: These detailed, relatable accounts not only inspire but also educate readers, showing them what to expect and how E M D R can lead to profound shifts in perspective and emotional well-being.

3. Motivation to Begin or Continue Therapy

For readers who feel uncertain about starting E M D R or discouraged by their current progress, these success stories serve as a powerful motivator. By illustrating that **healing is a process with ups and downs**, the book reassures readers that obstacles are normal and surmountable.

What Readers Will Gain:

- **Encouragement to Start**: Seeing others with similar struggles succeed reduces the fear of the unknown.
- **Validation During Setbacks**: Stories include challenges faced during therapy, normalizing setbacks and highlighting how individuals overcame them.
- **Inspiration for Progress**: The transformative outcomes show readers what is possible, sparking hope and determination.

Why It Stands Out: The stories instill confidence and motivation, reminding readers that every step forward, no matter how small, is a victory.

4. Emphasis on the Universality of Healing

The book emphasizes that healing through E M D R is not limited to specific types of trauma or emotional pain. By including success stories from varied contexts, it underscores the **versatility and adaptability of E M D R therapy**.

Highlighted Themes:

- Healing is possible regardless of the type or severity of trauma.
- E M D R is effective for both long-term, deeply rooted issues and more recent, situational stressors.
- Individuals from all walks of life—different ages, professions, and cultural backgrounds—have benefited from E M D R.

Why It Stands Out: This universal approach ensures that readers, regardless of their personal circumstances, feel included and hopeful about their own potential for healing.

5. Demonstrating Lasting Impact

The success stories highlight not just immediate relief but also the **long-term benefits of E M D R therapy**, showcasing how individuals' lives have changed in meaningful ways after completing therapy.

What Readers Will See:

- **Personal Growth**: Increased self-esteem, reduced self-doubt, and greater emotional regulation.
- **Improved Relationships**: Rebuilding trust, setting boundaries, and fostering healthier connections.

- **Life-Changing Milestones**: Overcoming fears to achieve professional success, find new hobbies, or embrace new relationships.
- **Resilience**: Stories of individuals who, after healing, use their experiences to help others, such as veterans mentoring fellow soldiers or parents building stronger families.

Why It Stands Out: By focusing on both immediate and long-term transformations, the book demonstrates that E M D R is not just about recovery but also about thriving in life.

6. Stories That Break Stigma

Mental health struggles and trauma often carry a stigma that prevents individuals from seeking help. These success stories break down barriers by openly discussing the emotions, challenges, and triumphs experienced during therapy.

What Readers Will Gain:

- A sense of normalcy regarding their own struggles.
- Validation that seeking therapy is a courageous and empowering step.
- Awareness that healing is a shared human experience, not a sign of weakness.

Why It Stands Out: The relatable nature of these stories reduces feelings of shame or isolation, encouraging readers to take the first step toward their own healing.

7. Hope for Every Stage of the Journey

Whether a reader is just beginning therapy, actively engaging in E M D R, or reflecting on their progress, these stories provide guidance and reassurance tailored to every stage of the healing process.

What Readers Will Find:

- **For Beginners**: Stories emphasize that therapy is a safe space to explore emotions and that progress is possible even if the journey feels daunting at first.
- **For Those in Progress**: Accounts of individuals overcoming setbacks, such as resistance or emotional overwhelm, offer strategies and motivation.
- **For Those Reflecting**: Narratives of individuals embracing their newfound freedom and resilience inspire readers to consider how their growth can shape their future.

Why It Stands Out: The stories meet readers where they are, providing hope and encouragement tailored to their specific stage of healing.

What Readers Will Gain

Through these diverse and relatable success stories, readers will:

- **Feel Inspired**: Witnessing the courage and transformation of others fosters hope and determination.
- **Find Validation**: Knowing that others have faced similar struggles normalizes their emotions and experiences.
- **Gain Insight**: Detailed accounts illustrate the practical and emotional aspects of E M D R therapy, helping readers understand what to expect.
- **Build Confidence**: Stories demonstrate that healing is achievable, regardless of the nature or severity of the trauma.
- **Feel Empowered**: The book reassures readers that they are not alone and that their journey, however challenging, is worth pursuing.

Chapter 12: Advanced E M D R Techniques

For those who have gained familiarity with the foundational practices of Eye Movement Desensitization and Reprocessing (E M D R), exploring advanced techniques can deepen and enhance the therapeutic experience. Advanced E M D R techniques are particularly beneficial for addressing complex trauma, chronic conditions, and intricate emotional or relational patterns. This chapter introduces readers to specialized approaches and modifications to the standard E M D R protocol, providing insights into how these methods can unlock deeper healing and tackle challenging therapeutic scenarios.

1. Targeting Complex Trauma with the Fractional Approach

What is the Fractional Approach?

Complex trauma often involves layers of interconnected memories, making it challenging to process all at once. The fractional approach involves breaking down these memories into smaller, more manageable components.

How It Works:

- The therapist identifies overarching themes, such as abandonment or betrayal.
- Instead of processing a full memory, specific elements (e.g., a facial expression, a phrase, or a physical sensation) are targeted.
- Bilateral stimulation (BLS) is used to reduce the emotional intensity of these fragments.

Benefits:

- Allows clients to process trauma without becoming overwhelmed.

- Creates emotional stability by addressing manageable parts of the experience.

Example: A client with a history of childhood abuse may begin by focusing on a single memory of hearing an angry tone, rather than the entire abusive incident. This gradual approach builds resilience for addressing deeper layers of trauma.

2. The Flash Technique for High Distress Memories

What is the Flash Technique?

The Flash Technique is a modified E M D R approach designed for processing memories that are too distressing to face directly. It uses rapid, indirect exposure to desensitize highly charged memories.

How It Works:

1. The client is asked to think about a neutral or pleasant memory while subtly "flashing" back to the traumatic memory for brief moments.
2. BLS is used during this process to reprocess the distress without fully engaging with the traumatic content.

Benefits:

- Reduces the emotional charge of overwhelming memories.
- Ideal for clients who feel unsafe or unable to revisit certain traumas.

Example: A client struggling with a severe car accident may focus on a calming beach scene while briefly and indirectly recalling aspects of the accident, such as the sound of brakes or the sight of shattered glass.

3. Using E M D R for Chronic Pain Management
How E M D R Addresses Pain:

Chronic pain often has psychological components, including emotional trauma or stress that amplifies physical sensations. Advanced E M D R techniques target the emotional underpinnings of pain, helping to reframe the brain's perception of discomfort.

Techniques:

- **Pain Mapping**:
  - The therapist guides the client to identify and describe the physical sensations of pain (e.g., "a sharp ache in my lower back").
  - BLS is used to process the emotional memories or beliefs tied to the pain (e.g., "I'm stuck with this forever").
- **Somatic Focus**:
  - Clients engage in BLS while focusing on the bodily sensation of pain, allowing the brain to reprocess its intensity and meaning.

Benefits:

- Reduces the emotional burden of chronic pain.
- Often leads to decreased physical discomfort.

Example: A client with fibromyalgia works on memories of feeling unsupported during their illness. As these emotions are processed, their perception of pain diminishes, improving their quality of life.

4. E M D R for Attachment and Relational Healing

What is **Attachment**-Focused E M D R?

Attachment-focused E M D R addresses the impact of early relational trauma, such as neglect or inconsistent caregiving, which can affect a person's ability to form healthy relationships.

How It Works:

- **Resource Development**: Therapists help clients build "internal resources," such as visualizing a nurturing caregiver or imagining themselves as a safe, supportive figure.
- **Processing Relational Memories**: E M D R targets key attachment injuries, such as moments of rejection or abandonment, and reprocesses the associated emotions and beliefs.

Benefits:

- Enhances trust, intimacy, and emotional security in relationships.
- Helps clients overcome patterns of avoidance, fear of abandonment, or over-dependence.

Example: A client with a fear of intimacy processes a childhood memory of being left alone during a difficult moment. Reframing this memory helps them approach relationships with greater confidence and trust.

5. The Cognitive Interweave for Stuck Points

What is the Cognitive Interweave?

The Cognitive Interweave is an advanced E M D R technique used when a client becomes "stuck" during reprocessing, unable to shift from a negative belief to a positive one.

How It Works:

- The therapist introduces logical, compassionate insights or reframes to help the client move forward.
- Examples include questions like, "What would you say to a friend in your situation?" or "What evidence do you have that this belief is true?"

Benefits:

- Breaks through cognitive blocks during reprocessing.
- Encourages new perspectives that align with healing.

Example: A client stuck on the belief "It was my fault" after a traumatic event may be prompted to consider, "What if the responsibility lies with someone else?" This new perspective allows the memory to be processed more effectively.

6. Future Template Technique for Resilience
What is the Future Template Technique?

This technique helps clients prepare for future challenges by "rehearsing" adaptive responses using E M D R.

How It Works:

1. The client identifies an upcoming situation that causes anxiety, such as a job interview or confrontation.
2. The therapist guides the client to visualize handling the situation with confidence and calmness.
3. BLS reinforces this visualization, creating a sense of readiness and emotional stability.

Benefits:

- Builds confidence and reduces anxiety about future events.
- Helps integrate positive beliefs into everyday life.

Example: A client preparing for a public speaking event practices visualizing themselves delivering a confident presentation. E M D R strengthens this image, reducing their fear and boosting their performance.

7. Resource Tapping for Emotional Stability
What is Resource Tapping?

Resource tapping is a self-soothing E M D R technique that helps clients stabilize emotions between sessions or during high-stress moments.

How It Works:

- Clients identify positive resources, such as feelings of safety, love, or calmness, and focus on them while engaging in BLS.
- This technique can involve tapping on knees, shoulders, or thighs while thinking of a "safe place" or a supportive memory.

Benefits:

- Provides immediate emotional regulation.
- Empowers clients to manage stress independently.

Example: A client feeling overwhelmed during a family gathering uses resource tapping to focus on a memory of hiking in the mountains, creating a sense of calm and safety.

8. E M D R with Imaginal Interweave
What is the Imaginal Interweave?

This technique involves creating a mental dialogue or imagery to resolve unresolved feelings or beliefs tied to a traumatic memory.

How It Works:

- The client imagines confronting a past abuser, setting boundaries, or receiving support they didn't have at the time.
- BLS reinforces the emotional resolution created through these imagined scenarios.

Benefits:

- Addresses unmet needs from past experiences.
- Helps clients process feelings of anger, sadness, or helplessness.

Example: A client who felt abandoned by a parent imagines their adult self comforting their younger self. This visualization creates a sense of closure and emotional healing.

9. Using E M D R for Generational Trauma

How It Works:

Generational trauma refers to emotional pain passed down through families. Advanced E M D R techniques help clients process not only their own memories but also inherited beliefs or emotions tied to family history.

- **Identifying Patterns**: Clients explore recurring themes, such as fear of failure or mistrust, that may originate from previous generations.
- **Processing with E M D R**: Specific memories or symbols representing generational trauma are reprocessed to release emotional burdens.

Benefits:

- Breaks cycles of trauma within families.
- Promotes healing across generations.

Example: A client struggling with a pervasive sense of guilt explores family stories of hardship and sacrifice, reprocessing these narratives to embrace their own freedom and individuality.

What Readers Will Learn

- How to use advanced E M D R techniques for addressing complex trauma, phobias, chronic pain, and relational challenges.
- Tools like the Fractional Approach, Flash Technique, and Cognitive Interweave for navigating stuck points and difficult emotions.
- Methods for building emotional stability, preparing for future challenges, and addressing generational trauma.
- Practical ways to integrate these techniques into their healing journey, enhancing resilience and long-term growth.

What Readers Will Learn: A Look into Specialized E M D R Techniques Like the Flash Technique and Other Advanced Practices

This chapter delves into the **specialized techniques and advanced practices in E M D R therapy** that go beyond the standard protocol. Readers will gain an in-depth understanding of innovative approaches like the **Flash Technique**, along with other advanced methods tailored for addressing complex trauma, overwhelming distress, and specific therapeutic challenges. These techniques offer a more nuanced and flexible way to harness the power of E M D R, providing tools to tackle deeply rooted emotional wounds, enhance emotional stability, and ensure a smoother healing journey.

1. The Flash Technique: A Gentle Approach for High-Distress Memories

The Flash Technique is a cutting-edge E M D R method designed to help clients process extremely distressing memories without directly engaging with their full emotional intensity. This technique is particularly useful for individuals who feel unsafe or overwhelmed by the prospect of revisiting their trauma.

How It Works:

- **Indirect Exposure**: The client focuses on a pleasant or neutral thought while "flashing" brief awareness of the traumatic memory.
- **Bilateral Stimulation (BLS)**: BLS is applied while the client alternates between the positive focus and the traumatic memory, allowing the brain to reprocess the memory in a non-threatening way.
- **Gradual Desensitization**: Over time, the emotional intensity of the traumatic memory diminishes without requiring the client to fully confront it.

Applications:

- Ideal for clients with severe P T S D or extreme phobias.
- Useful for processing memories that are too painful to address directly, such as abuse or loss.

What Readers Will Learn:

- How the Flash Technique minimizes emotional overwhelm while facilitating healing.
- Why it is particularly effective for trauma survivors who feel "stuck" in their healing journey.
- Practical examples of how this method can be integrated into therapy sessions.

2. The Cognitive Interweave: Breaking Through Stuck Points

The Cognitive Interweave is an advanced E M D R tool used when clients encounter "stuck points" during reprocessing. These are moments when the client struggles to shift from a negative belief to a more adaptive and positive perspective.

How It Works:

- **Therapist-Guided Questions**: The therapist introduces logical or compassionate insights to help the client break through cognitive blocks.
- **Reframing Negative Beliefs**: Examples include prompting the client to consider, "What evidence supports this belief?" or "What would you tell a friend in your situation?"
- **BLS Integration**: These insights are paired with BLS to reinforce new, healthier perspectives.

Applications:

- Effective for clients with deeply ingrained negative beliefs, such as "I'm unlovable" or "I'll always fail."
- Helpful for addressing unresolved guilt, shame, or self-blame.

What Readers Will Learn:

- How the Cognitive Interweave helps clients challenge and replace rigid thought patterns.
- Techniques for integrating compassionate self-talk and rational analysis into E M D R sessions.
- Examples of how this approach accelerates progress in difficult cases.

3. Resource Development and Installation (RDI): Building Emotional Strength

RDI is an advanced E M D R technique that focuses on creating and reinforcing internal emotional resources before addressing traumatic memories. This practice ensures that clients have the tools they need to feel safe and grounded during therapy.

How It Works:

- **Identifying Strengths**: Clients work with their therapist to identify personal strengths, positive memories, or supportive figures (real or imagined).
- **Installing Resources**: BLS is used to reinforce these positive associations, making them more readily accessible during moments of stress.
- **Preparation for Reprocessing**: These resources act as a safety net, allowing clients to approach difficult memories with greater emotional stability.

Applications:

- Ideal for clients with high levels of emotional dysregulation or complex trauma.
- Useful for those who feel under-resourced or overwhelmed by the idea of therapy.

What Readers Will Learn:

- How to create a "safe place" and other emotional resources to manage stress and anxiety.
- Why RDI is essential for clients with a history of relational trauma or chronic instability.
- Step-by-step guidance on incorporating resource development into their healing journey.

4. The Fractional Approach: Processing Complex Trauma in Stages

Complex trauma often involves a series of interconnected memories and emotions that cannot be processed all at once. The fractional approach involves breaking down these memories into smaller, more manageable components.

How It Works:

- **Fragmented Targeting**: Instead of tackling an entire traumatic event, clients focus on smaller aspects, such as a specific sensation, sound, or image.
- **Gradual Progression**: Once the client feels more comfortable with smaller pieces of the memory, they can begin to address larger themes or patterns.
- **Building Tolerance**: This approach allows for incremental healing, minimizing emotional overwhelm.

Applications:

- Effective for clients with dissociative tendencies or extreme emotional sensitivity.
- Useful for addressing layered traumas, such as ongoing abuse or neglect.

What Readers Will Learn:

- How breaking trauma into smaller components can make therapy less daunting.
- Techniques for identifying which aspects of a memory to process first.
- Why the fractional approach builds emotional resilience and reduces the risk of retraumatization.

5. The Future Template: Preparing for Success

The Future Template technique is designed to help clients visualize and rehearse positive outcomes for future challenges. By reinforcing these scenarios with BLS, clients develop greater confidence and emotional readiness.

How It Works:

- **Identifying Future Challenges**: The client selects an upcoming situation that causes anxiety or uncertainty, such as a job interview or family gathering.
- **Visualizing Success**: The therapist guides the client to imagine handling the situation calmly and effectively.
- **BLS Reinforcement**: BLS is used to strengthen the positive emotions and beliefs associated with the visualization.

Applications:

- Helps clients who struggle with performance anxiety or fear of failure.
- Prepares individuals for life transitions, such as returning to work after trauma or starting new relationships.

What Readers Will Learn:

- How to use the Future Template to build emotional resilience and confidence.
- Why visualizing success can rewire the brain to approach challenges with optimism.
- Practical examples of applying this technique to everyday scenarios.

6. The Somatic-Focused Approach: Releasing Trauma Stored in the Body

Trauma often manifests physically, leading to chronic tension, pain, or other somatic symptoms. A somatic-focused E M D R approach addresses these bodily sensations alongside emotional memories.

How It Works:

- **Body Awareness**: The client identifies where they feel physical discomfort or tension related to trauma.
- **BLS for Physical Sensations**: The client focuses on these sensations during BLS, allowing the brain to reprocess their intensity and meaning.
- **Somatic Release**: Gentle movements, such as stretching or grounding exercises, are integrated into the session to facilitate physical release.

Applications:

- Ideal for clients with somatic conditions, such as chronic pain, or those with trauma stored in the body.
- Useful for addressing the mind-body connection in emotional healing.

What Readers Will Learn:

- How somatic-focused techniques help release physical manifestations of trauma.
- Methods for integrating body awareness and movement into E M D R sessions.
- Why addressing physical symptoms can accelerate emotional recovery.

7. Advanced Techniques for Generational Trauma

Generational trauma refers to patterns of emotional pain passed down through families. E M D R can be adapted to address inherited beliefs, fears, and behaviors.

How It Works:

- **Identifying Themes**: Clients explore family dynamics and recurring patterns, such as guilt, fear of failure, or perfectionism.
- **Symbolic Processing**: Symbols, such as family stories or cultural rituals, are used as targets for reprocessing.
- **Releasing Emotional Burdens**: E M D R helps clients let go of inherited trauma while honoring family connections.

Applications:

- Effective for clients who feel burdened by family expectations or unresolved generational conflicts.
- Helps break cycles of trauma for future generations.

What Readers Will Learn:

- How to recognize and address generational trauma through E M D R.
- Techniques for processing inherited beliefs and emotions.
- The role of E M D R in fostering healing across family systems.

Why It Stands Out: Highlights Innovative Tools Often Missing in Beginner-Focused Guides

This book distinguishes itself by offering **advanced and innovative E M D R techniques** that go beyond what typical beginner-focused guides offer. While most introductory resources focus on the foundational aspects of E M D R therapy, this book delves into **cutting-edge tools** and **specialized practices** designed to address complex trauma, enhance emotional resilience, and speed up recovery. These tools, such as the Flash Technique, Resource Development and Installation, and the Future Template, are often overlooked in more basic guides, yet they can dramatically improve the effectiveness and depth of therapy.

1. Advanced Techniques for Complex Trauma

Many beginner guides to E M D R focus primarily on the **eight phases of standard E M D R therapy** and may not explore the **advanced techniques** that can better address complex, multi-layered traumas like **complex P T S D, dissociative disorders**, or **chronic emotional wounds**. In contrast, this book offers a detailed exploration of how advanced methods like the **Flash Technique** and **Cognitive Interweave** can provide powerful tools for **highly sensitive or severely traumatized individuals**.

For example, the **Flash Technique**, which involves **briefly exposing clients to a traumatic memory while maintaining focus on a positive thought**, allows individuals who are too overwhelmed by the intensity of their trauma to heal at their own pace, minimizing the risk of retraumatization. It is a **gentle and effective approach**, often not covered in beginner guides, making this book a valuable resource for anyone who has encountered roadblocks in their healing process.

2. Emphasis on Somatic and Mind-Body Healing

Traditional E M D R techniques primarily focus on **emotional reprocessing**, often neglecting the **somatic aspects of trauma**. In this book, **somatic-focused E M D R techniques** are integrated into the framework, recognizing that trauma is not only an emotional experience but also a **physical one**. These advanced practices help clients release the **physical tension, chronic pain**, or **somatic symptoms** that often accompany unresolved trauma.

By incorporating techniques that address the **mind-body connection**, this book ensures that readers can treat trauma at its core, addressing both **psychological and physical symptoms** in ways beginner guides do not. Through **somatic awareness exercises** and targeted **bilateral stimulation (BLS)** for physical sensations, individuals can experience **full-body healing**, breaking the cycle of trauma that manifests both mentally and physically.

3. The Future Template: Preparing for Success

Another hallmark of this book is its inclusion of the **Future Template** technique, which is **rarely covered** in beginner-focused resources. The Future Template helps clients to **visualize and rehearse success** in upcoming challenges, whether they're related to **social anxiety, performance issues**, or **life transitions**.

While beginner guides typically focus on **processing past trauma**, the **Future Template** offers a forward-looking, **strengthening approach** that builds emotional resilience. It allows clients to actively prepare for future stressors with a **positive mindset**, reinforcing their **sense of control and confidence**. This proactive approach is essential for individuals looking to prevent future setbacks while **empowering them to move forward** from past trauma.

4. Tailored Approaches for Unique Cases

Unlike beginner guides that provide a **one-size-fits-all framework**, this book offers **customizable approaches** for unique therapeutic situations. Readers will learn how to tailor E M D R techniques to suit a variety of **trauma types**, from **childhood abuse** to **grief, relationship trauma**, and **identity struggles**. These specialized approaches allow therapists and clients to **personalize the healing process**, ensuring that therapy is as effective and relevant as possible.

For example, **generational trauma** is a significant aspect that many beginners overlook. This book teaches readers how to use E M D R to **break the cycle of inherited emotional wounds**, empowering clients to heal from **family patterns** that may have been passed down for generations. This insight into **family systems and generational healing** is **rarely found in introductory guides**, making it an invaluable resource for those seeking to break free from longstanding patterns.

5. Integration of E M D R with Other Therapies

Most beginner-focused books on E M D R focus on the therapy **in isolation**. However, this book goes beyond traditional methods by demonstrating how E M D R can be seamlessly **integrated with other therapeutic modalities**, such as **CBT, mindfulness, talk therapy**, and even **somatic experiencing**.

For readers who may already be familiar with one or more of these therapies, this integration is vital in creating a **holistic, multi-dimensional healing plan**. By learning how to combine E M D R with **other evidence-based treatments**, readers will gain a comprehensive toolkit for **addressing complex issues** that may not be fully resolved by any one modality. This integrated approach provides **greater flexibility and adaptability**, ensuring that readers can use the best tools available for their unique healing journey.

6. Real-Life Success Stories and Case Studies

What sets this book apart is its use of **real-life success stories** and **case studies** that provide concrete examples of how these advanced techniques work in practice. While many beginner guides may provide theoretical explanations, this book offers readers **practical examples of how these techniques unfold in real-world therapy sessions**.

Through these success stories, readers not only learn how **advanced E M D R tools** can help in various trauma scenarios but also gain **hope and inspiration** from others who have successfully healed. These **personal accounts** bridge the gap between theory and practice, making the content more relatable and empowering.

7. Self-Help and Empowerment

Finally, unlike beginner guides that often leave readers with limited practical tools, this book offers a wealth of **self-help techniques** that readers can use on their own. From **mindfulness exercises** to **grounding techniques**, the book ensures that individuals don't have to wait for a therapist to implement E M D R—they can begin the healing process **right away**. These **self-assessment tools**, checklists, and **guided exercises** are a **unique addition** that empowers readers to take charge of their own healing journey.

Chapter 13. E M D R for Kids and Teens

E M D R for Kids and Teens is a specialized approach to **Eye Movement Desensitization and Reprocessing** (E M D R) therapy designed specifically to meet the unique emotional and developmental needs of younger individuals. Adolescence is a time of tremendous emotional, physical, and social change, making it a period when trauma can deeply impact a person's growth. Whether it's due to bullying, family dysfunction, abuse, grief, or other traumatic experiences, young people can experience lasting emotional scars. E M D R for kids and teens offers a **compassionate and adaptable therapeutic model** that allows them to process and heal these emotional wounds.

This chapter will provide a comprehensive exploration of how E M D R is applied in the context of child and adolescent therapy. It will cover the **specific adaptations** needed for younger clients, how E M D R can address the unique challenges that children and teens face, and why it's a highly effective treatment for young trauma survivors.

What Readers Will Learn:

1. E M D R's Effectiveness for Children and Teens

E M D R's core principles—bilateral stimulation and reprocessing of traumatic memories—can be profoundly effective for children and teens. However, younger individuals often need an approach that is **developmentally appropriate** and tailored to their cognitive, emotional, and social stage of development.

Readers will learn how E M D R therapists can modify the standard eight-phase protocol to engage with younger clients in ways that help them process memories **at their own pace**. For example, while an adult may be able to articulate a traumatic memory and its emotional impact, a child may need to use **creative techniques**, such as **drawing, storytelling, or play therapy**, to process and express their feelings. In these cases, the therapist may guide the child to represent the traumatic experience through art, which can be just as effective as verbal processing.

2. Age-Appropriate Tools and Techniques

Children and teens are not only developmentally different from adults—they also face different life stressors. For instance, a 5-year-old might experience trauma from witnessing a car accident, while a 16-year-old may struggle with issues of **peer pressure, bullying, or body image**. E M D R for kids and teens requires modifications to make the process **engaging, accessible, and comfortable** for the younger demographic.

In this section, readers will discover a variety of **age-appropriate tools** and techniques used in E M D R therapy for younger clients, including:

- **Imaginal Play and Storytelling:** For children, the therapist might ask them to create a story about their trauma or have them imagine a character going through a similar experience. This method allows children to distance themselves from the emotional intensity of the memory while still working through it.
- **Safe Place and Positive Imagery:** Children are taught to create a "safe place" in their minds where they can feel calm and grounded, especially during times of intense emotional overwhelm. This imagery is often reinforced through drawing or visualizations, helping them engage with their emotions safely.
- **Sensory Integration:** E M D R uses **bilateral stimulation** (BLS), typically in the form of eye movements, but this can be difficult for younger children to maintain. Instead, therapists may use **tactile stimulation** like tapping or hand-held buzzers, or **auditory cues** like alternating sounds.

- **Interactive Techniques:** For teens, E M D R may integrate **music, video clips, or journaling** to help them identify and process traumatic memories. Teens are often more verbal and can engage with the therapy using tools that resonate with their lifestyle.

3. Common Issues in Treating Kids and Teens with E M D R

While E M D R can be incredibly effective for younger clients, it's essential to recognize that certain **challenges** are unique to children and adolescents. These include **difficulty articulating emotions, limited coping skills**, and **issues with attention or focus** that may arise during the therapy process.

In this section, readers will gain insight into how therapists can address these challenges:

- **Building Rapport:** Establishing a solid, trust-based relationship with young clients is key to the success of E M D R. This chapter will highlight the importance of **creativity** and **flexibility** in therapy to make sure that the child feels understood and safe.
- **Overcoming Distractibility:** Younger children, especially those with ADHD or other focus-related difficulties, may struggle with the concentration required for standard E M D R techniques. Therapists must be **patient** and **adaptive**, possibly using shorter sessions, offering breaks, or using highly engaging tools like toys or games to help keep the child's attention focused.
- **Addressing Family Dynamics:** For many children and teens, trauma is deeply intertwined with **family issues** (e.g., divorce, conflict, or parental addiction). Therapy may also need to address **family systems**, so the child feels supported at home during the healing process.

4. The Role of Parents and Caregivers

An essential component of E M D R therapy for children and teens is the involvement of **parents and caregivers**. While E M D R can work effectively on its own, the support system plays a critical role in the child's **ongoing healing** outside of therapy sessions. In this section, readers will learn:

- **How to Involve Parents in the Process:** This chapter outlines how parents can **reinforce positive changes** made during therapy, provide a safe environment for emotional expression, and help monitor the child's progress.
- **Guidelines for Supporting the Child at Home:** Parents will learn ways to manage the child's emotional responses post-session, as sometimes **processing trauma** can lead to **temporary emotional distress**.
- **Self-Care for Parents:** E M D R therapy can be intense for both the child and the caregiver. This section provides practical advice on **how parents can manage their own emotional reactions** during the process to provide the best support for their child's healing journey.

What Readers Will Learn: Adapting E M D R for Younger Audiences to Address Childhood Trauma, Bullying, or Anxiety

In this section, readers will discover how **E M D R** (Eye Movement Desensitization and Reprocessing) can be effectively adapted for **younger audiences**, specifically for addressing childhood trauma, bullying, or anxiety. While E M D R is primarily used in adult therapy, it has been shown to be highly effective for children and adolescents when tailored to their developmental needs. Through a combination of **age-appropriate techniques** and **creative interventions**, E M D R can provide lasting relief for young individuals struggling with emotional pain, anxiety, and trauma.

1. Adapting E M D R for Children and Teens

While the core principles of E M D R remain the same for all age groups, applying them to children and teens requires thoughtful adjustments. In this chapter, readers will gain insights into **adapting E M D R protocols** for a younger population, ensuring that they can benefit from this powerful therapy in ways that are **relatable**, **comfortable**, and **developmentally suitable**.

Techniques Tailored to Age and Cognitive Development:

- **Child-Friendly Communication:** For younger children, therapists often use simple, direct language and avoid technical terms that might be confusing. For example, instead of discussing the "desensitization" process, therapists may say something like "We're going to help your brain feel better about the thing that makes you scared or sad."
- **Creative Interventions:** Children, especially younger ones, often struggle to express emotions verbally. E M D R for children can include methods such as **drawing**, **playing with toys**, or **storytelling** to help process their emotions. These methods allow children to express themselves in a more accessible way. For example, a child might draw a picture of their trauma, or they could imagine a superhero who is "fighting" the negative feelings associated with their experience.
- **Play Therapy Integration:** Play is a child's natural language, and therapists may incorporate **play-based activities** during E M D R. Using toys, games, or even imaginative play, therapists can help children articulate their trauma experiences in non-verbal ways. Play therapy helps the child distance themselves

from the trauma while still processing the emotions involved.

2. Addressing Specific Types of Childhood Trauma

E M D R is particularly effective for treating **trauma-related disorders** that stem from a variety of childhood experiences, such as **abuse, bullying**, or **neglect**. In this section, readers will learn how E M D R can specifically target and address these types of trauma.

Childhood Trauma:

- **Sexual Abuse or Physical Abuse:** For children who have experienced abuse, E M D R can help **desensitize** the painful memories while facilitating the reprocessing of those memories in a way that reduces their emotional charge. For young children, therapists will work to make the process as non-threatening as possible, often incorporating elements of **safe space imagery** to ensure the child feels in control.
- **Witnessing Violence:** Children who witness violence or other forms of trauma, such as domestic violence or an accident, often suffer from **secondary trauma**. E M D R helps them process these traumatic events by targeting the images, thoughts, and feelings they have associated with the event. Therapists may use **visualization** techniques, asking the child to imagine the trauma as a movie, which they can later "change" or "edit" in the safe space of their mind.
- **Separation and Loss:** The trauma of a parent's death, divorce, or a breakup can be deeply painful. E M D R allows the child to process feelings of abandonment, loss, or grief by identifying the **core memories** associated with these events. Through this, the child can learn healthier ways to cope and reframe the trauma in a more adaptive way.

3. Managing Bullying Trauma

One of the most common and distressing forms of trauma for children and teens is **bullying**. Whether it's physical, verbal, or cyberbullying, the emotional scars from such experiences can linger long after the bullying stops. In this chapter, readers will explore how E M D R can be particularly effective for helping children and teens heal from **bullying trauma**.

Reprocessing Bullying Memories:

- **Identification of Negative Beliefs:** Children and teens who have been bullied often internalize negative beliefs about themselves, such as "I'm not good enough" or "I don't belong." E M D R helps these young clients reprocess the traumatic memories linked to bullying, **challenging** these negative beliefs and replacing them with healthier, more **empowering thoughts**.
- **Processing the Emotional Impact:** E M D R allows the therapist to help the child revisit bullying memories, helping them identify their **emotional reactions** to the event (e.g., sadness, anger, shame). By using **bilateral stimulation** to guide the brain's natural healing process, children are able to reprocess these painful emotions in a way that reduces their intensity.
- **Empowering the Child:** Through E M D R, children are not only able to reframe their trauma, but also **reclaim a sense of power and control** over their emotional responses. As they process these difficult memories, they can develop a stronger sense of **self-worth** and resilience.

4. Alleviating Anxiety in Children and Teens

Anxiety is one of the most common mental health struggles among children and adolescents. Whether it's social anxiety, performance anxiety, or generalized anxiety, E M D R can help young clients process the **triggers** behind their anxiety and develop healthier coping mechanisms.

E M D R Techniques for Managing Anxiety:

- **Desensitization of Anxiety Triggers:** Children and teens who experience frequent anxiety attacks often have specific **triggers**—certain situations, thoughts, or memories that provoke overwhelming feelings. E M D R helps identify and desensitize these triggers, reducing their emotional charge and teaching the child how to remain calm and grounded.
- **Creating Calm and Safe Places:** One of the first steps in E M D R therapy is often to establish a **safe place** in the child's mind—a space where they can go whenever they feel anxious or afraid. This visualization can serve as a comforting tool, allowing the child to feel in control when confronted with anxiety-inducing situations.
- **Self-Regulation Skills:** As part of the therapeutic process, readers will learn how E M D R can teach children and teens important self-regulation skills. These skills, such as **deep breathing**, **mindfulness**, or **visualization**, help kids manage their anxiety independently.

5. Why E M D R Works for Kids and Teens

In this section, readers will understand why E M D R is such an effective therapeutic model for younger individuals. E M D R taps into the brain's natural ability to heal emotional wounds, and when used with younger clients, it allows them to process trauma in a **gentle, adaptable way**. Unlike traditional talk therapy, which might be difficult for children who lack the vocabulary to express their emotions, E M D R allows them to process trauma through **non-verbal** means and **creative outlets**. Additionally, the **bilateral stimulation** used in E M D R helps to activate both sides of the brain, promoting **integration** of the traumatic memory and supporting healing in a holistic way.

Why It Stands Out: Includes Unique Content for Parents and Teachers That Competitors Might Not Have

This section distinguishes your book by offering **targeted, practical guidance for parents, teachers, and other caregivers**—a demographic often overlooked in other E M D R-related books. While many guides focus solely on the therapeutic process from a professional's perspective, this book uniquely integrates the roles of **parents** and **teachers** in the healing journey of children and teens undergoing E M D R therapy. By addressing the critical **supportive roles** these individuals play, the book ensures that the healing process is more holistic, accessible, and effective for young clients.

1. Parent's Role in Supporting E M D R Therapy

Parents are often the primary emotional support for children and teens, making their involvement crucial in the success of E M D R therapy. In this section, readers will learn how **parents can create a nurturing environment** at home to enhance the effects of E M D R therapy. The book provides actionable, easy-to-implement advice that parents can use to **support their child's emotional well-being** before, during, and after sessions.

Guidance for Parents:

- **Creating a Safe and Supportive Home Environment:** Parents are encouraged to set up a **calm and secure home atmosphere**, which is essential for helping children process difficult emotions. Tips include reducing unnecessary stressors, ensuring regular routines, and fostering an environment where the child feels heard and supported.

- **How to Engage in Conversations About Trauma:** Parents often struggle with knowing how to talk to their children about trauma. This book provides **age-appropriate communication strategies**, helping parents ask open-ended questions and offer reassurance without pushing their child to share before they are ready.
- **Building Emotional Resilience at Home:** Parents can actively engage in strengthening their child's emotional resilience. Techniques such as **deep breathing exercises**, **mindfulness practices**, and **positive affirmations** are included to help parents guide their children in managing stress and emotional upheaval between therapy sessions.

Empowering Parents for Long-Term Success:

The book also highlights the **long-term nature of trauma healing** and the **importance of parental consistency**. It outlines how parents can **monitor progress**, maintain a **consistent dialogue**, and be **patient** as their child undergoes the healing process. By offering examples of how to deal with setbacks and emotional reactions, the book ensures that parents feel **empowered** to support their child over the course of therapy.

2. Teacher's Role in Supporting E M D R Therapy

While teachers may not be trained in E M D R, they play an indispensable role in a child's emotional and academic recovery. This book highlights **how teachers can support emotional healing** and **reduce stress in the classroom** for children undergoing E M D R therapy. The strategies offered are designed to be **practical and actionable**, ensuring that teachers can create an emotionally safe environment conducive to healing.

Supportive Strategies for Teachers:

- **Recognizing Signs of Trauma in the Classroom:** Teachers are often the first to notice if a child is struggling with **anxiety, distractibility**, or **emotional outbursts**. This book teaches teachers how to identify potential signs of trauma or anxiety in students and how to approach these behaviors with **empathy and understanding**.
- **Creating Trauma-Sensitive Learning Environments:** The book provides practical advice on how teachers can make their classrooms more **trauma-sensitive**. This includes incorporating **relaxation techniques** into daily routines, such as mindful moments before tests, or allowing children to use **safe spaces** to decompress when feeling overwhelmed.
- **Supporting Emotional Healing Without Overstepping:** Teachers are given the tools to recognize their limits—E M D R is a therapeutic process, and teachers are not expected to do therapy themselves. Instead, they are encouraged to be **active allies** by collaborating with parents and therapists to ensure that they are supporting the child's emotional needs without pushing them too far. For example, teachers might help monitor a child's **emotional responses** to stress and work closely with therapists to adapt the child's academic workload to match their emotional state.

Classroom Strategies to Empower Students:

Teachers are shown how to create **emotional support plans** for students, integrating trauma-informed practices into the school environment. These strategies may include **calming strategies**, **mindfulness exercises**, and **positive reinforcement** that can help students feel more secure and motivated while at school.

3. Collaborative Effort Between Parents, Teachers, and Therapists

The integration of these **two key support systems**—parents and teachers—into the E M D R healing process sets this book apart from others. While many books focus solely on the **therapist's** role, this book offers clear, specific guidance for **cross-collaboration** between parents, teachers, and therapists to create a unified, **consistent healing approach**.

Building a Healing Support Team:

- **Communication and Cooperation:** This section teaches readers how to set up open lines of communication between **therapists, parents**, and **teachers** to ensure a cohesive and well-rounded treatment plan for the child. For example, parents and teachers can be trained to recognize when a child is struggling with certain triggers and work in tandem with therapists to address them.
- **Sharing Goals and Tracking Progress:** The book introduces **tracking tools** such as **progress journals** or **feedback forms** for teachers and parents to use when they notice specific patterns of behavior. By working together, this trio of support creates a continuous feedback loop that encourages growth.
- **Customized Healing Plans:** Every child's needs are different, and this book shows how **parents**, **teachers**, and **therapists** can customize support plans that are flexible and tailored to the child's specific emotional journey. With case studies and examples, readers can see how this team-based approach works in real-life scenarios.

4. Empowering Support Systems for Long-Term Success

By targeting the essential roles of **parents** and **teachers**, this book empowers readers to create a **collaborative, nurturing network** around children undergoing E M D R therapy. This network can continue to support the child well after therapy ends, creating a **sustained healing environment** that aids the child in processing trauma long-term. Readers will learn how to be **advocates for their children's mental health**, helping children thrive both emotionally and academically.

Chapter 14. E M D R and Cultural Sensitivity

In trauma healing, **cultural sensitivity** is a crucial but often overlooked aspect, especially when applying therapeutic techniques like **Eye Movement Desensitization and Reprocessing (E M D R)**. As therapy becomes increasingly diverse and globally accessible, it's essential that mental health professionals, as well as self-healers and individuals practicing E M D R techniques independently, understand how **cultural identity** and **values** intersect with trauma and healing. This chapter provides a comprehensive exploration of **cultural sensitivity** in the context of E M D R, helping readers understand how different cultural backgrounds, beliefs, and practices can impact the trauma recovery process.

What Readers Will Learn

- **The Role of Cultural Identity in Trauma:** The book explores how **cultural background**, including ethnicity, religion, and social upbringing, can shape an individual's experience of trauma and their approach to healing. For example, a person from a collectivist culture may approach healing as a communal process, whereas someone from an individualistic culture may value personal independence in therapy.
- **Culturally Informed E M D R Practices:** This section provides readers with a detailed framework for incorporating **cultural awareness** into their E M D R practice. Whether a client is working with a therapist or practicing self-E M D R, understanding the cultural influences on emotional wounds can improve therapy outcomes.
- **Overcoming Cultural Barriers to Therapy:** Many people, especially those from marginalized or minority backgrounds, may experience hesitancy or

mistrust towards therapeutic approaches due to **historical stigmas**, **cultural taboos**, or negative past experiences with medical professionals. Readers will learn how to **recognize these barriers** and actively work to **reduce resistance** by integrating culturally sensitive practices into the therapy process.

- **Adapting E M D R to Different Cultural Contexts:** E M D R, while based on universally effective principles, can be **tailored** to be more effective when cultural elements, such as **family dynamics**, **spirituality**, or **rituals**, are considered. This chapter includes practical ways of adapting E M D R techniques to make them more accessible, relevant, and resonant with individuals from diverse backgrounds.

Why Cultural Sensitivity Matters in E M D R

Trauma is a **universal experience**, but the way it is **perceived, processed**, and **expressed** varies greatly depending on cultural and societal influences. When trauma occurs within a particular cultural context, it is often embedded in **historical, social, and community-based narratives** that can influence how individuals view their pain, express their emotions, and engage with healing practices.

1. Understanding Trauma Across Cultures

Cultural beliefs shape the way **trauma** is defined and understood. For example:

- In many **Western societies**, trauma is often defined through the lens of **individual experiences**, such as **personal assault**, **grief**, or **accidents**. Here, trauma is typically addressed through **individual therapy**, focusing on personal healing and self-reflection.

- However, in cultures where **family** or **community** is central, trauma may be perceived as a **family or group issue**, and the healing process may require involvement from the larger community or spiritual leaders. This can include practices like **community rituals**, **family counseling**, or **spiritual ceremonies**, all of which should be acknowledged and respected in the E M D R process.

Cultural understanding can also change the way symptoms manifest. For example, trauma in some cultures may manifest in **somatic symptoms** (e.g., pain or illness) rather than emotional or psychological symptoms. Recognizing this can help the therapist or practitioner **adapt their approach** to ensure that **somatic-based trauma** is effectively addressed through E M D R.

2. Cultural Competency in Practicing E M D R

Cultural competency refers to the ability to **understand**, **respect**, and **interact effectively** with people from different cultures. Practicing E M D R with cultural sensitivity means more than just recognizing cultural differences; it involves integrating those differences into the therapeutic process.

- **Language Sensitivity:** E M D R involves deep emotional processing, which can be difficult to articulate in a non-native language or when words do not directly translate. Therapists must be **mindful of language barriers** and use **culturally appropriate metaphors**, stories, or language. For instance, in some cultures, certain terms for emotions may not exist or may be understood differently. A skilled practitioner will know how to navigate these nuances.
- **Holistic Healing:** In many cultures, **spirituality** plays an integral role in trauma healing. Some individuals may turn to **faith healers** or religious

leaders in times of distress. Incorporating the person's **spiritual beliefs** into the E M D R process, whether through **prayer**, **meditation**, or **ceremonies**, can facilitate a deeper connection to the healing process.

- **Rituals and Symbols:** Many cultures place importance on rituals and symbols as tools for healing. E M D R practitioners can honor these elements by incorporating **cultural symbols** into the healing process (e.g., offering culturally significant objects or imagery during the **bilateral stimulation** process) to make the therapy experience feel more connected to the client's lived reality.

Challenges of Cultural Sensitivity in E M D R

While integrating cultural sensitivity into E M D R therapy is essential, it does come with challenges:

1. Overcoming Stereotypes and Assumptions

It's crucial to avoid assuming that a person's cultural background defines their emotional or psychological experiences. Cultural sensitivity requires **active listening**, without jumping to conclusions or applying stereotypes. For instance, a therapist may need to be aware of cultural **differences in emotional expression**—in some cultures, **stoicism** or **reserved emotional responses** might be seen as a sign of **strength**, while in others, **outward expressions of emotion** might be more culturally encouraged.

2. Finding Culturally Appropriate Tools

While **standard E M D R protocols** are effective for many, they may need to be adapted to meet the needs of individuals from specific cultural contexts. For example, the **cognitive interweaving** process, a central part of E M D R, may involve **metaphors** that are culturally relevant to the client's worldview. If a client has grown up in a culture that values communal interdependence, metaphors of **community strength** or **healing together** might resonate more than individualistic symbols.

Key Takeaways: How E M D R Supports Cultural Sensitivity

- **Cultural Awareness in Therapy:** Understanding that trauma is **experienced differently** across cultures and societies ensures that E M D R can be applied in a way that respects the client's worldview.
- **Tailored Healing Approaches:** The principles of E M D R can be **customized** to incorporate cultural practices, family dynamics, and spiritual beliefs, making therapy feel more relevant and personal to the client.
- **Collaboration with the Client's Cultural Environment:** A culturally sensitive E M D R practitioner understands the importance of collaboration with the individual's **support network**, which may include spiritual leaders, family members, or community figures.
- **Navigating Potential Barriers:** This chapter addresses common **cultural challenges** such as mistrust of therapy, language barriers, or a preference for non-traditional healing methods, and offers practical strategies to overcome them.

What Readers Will Learn: How to Adapt E M D R for People from Diverse Cultural Backgrounds

When applying **Eye Movement Desensitization and Reprocessing (E M D R)** to individuals from diverse cultural backgrounds, it's essential to understand that **culture** plays a significant role in how people experience and process trauma. Trauma is universally felt, but the way it is **expressed**, **processed**, and **healed** can differ greatly depending on cultural contexts, values, and norms. In this section, readers will gain the tools and knowledge necessary to **adapt E M D R therapy** in ways that honor cultural differences and improve therapeutic outcomes for individuals from all walks of life.

1. Understanding the Role of Culture in Trauma Processing

Before diving into specific adaptations of E M D R, it's important to recognize how **cultural influences** shape the **experience of trauma**. Each culture has its own **ways of understanding emotional pain**, **expressing distress**, and **coping with hardship**. These cultural elements significantly impact how individuals view their emotional wounds and engage with therapeutic modalities like E M D R.

- **Cultural Definitions of Trauma:** Different cultures may define trauma in varying ways. For example, in some communities, trauma may not be limited to **personal events** like accidents or assaults but could include **communal suffering**, such as **loss of collective identity**, **displacement**, or **historical trauma** (e.g., colonization, slavery). E M D R practitioners need to broaden their definition of trauma to encompass these collective and socio-cultural factors, allowing them to address a wider array of emotional wounds.
- **Expression of Emotions:** Some cultures encourage **stoicism** or emotional restraint, while others prioritize **emotional expression** and **openness**. These differences will influence how clients may engage with E M D R techniques, such as the **Bilateral Stimulation (BLS)**, and how they may express distress during or after a session. Adapting E M D R to allow for **personal comfort** with emotional expression is crucial.

2. Culturally Tailoring E M D R's Standard Protocols

While **E M D R** operates on the same fundamental principles worldwide, the application of its protocols can be adjusted to better meet the needs of clients from specific cultural backgrounds. Here's how:

A. Building Trust Through Cultural Competence

For any therapy to be successful, establishing **trust** is paramount. Cultural competence means being able to navigate and respect a client's **beliefs**, **values**, and **experiences** while also recognizing the historical and cultural contexts that might shape their perception of therapy.

- **Understanding Cultural Barriers:** For example, individuals from certain cultures may harbor **mistrust** toward mental health professionals, especially in cultures where seeking professional help is stigmatized or viewed as a sign of weakness. In such cases, the therapist must be aware of these potential barriers and use culturally sensitive methods to build rapport and make the process of therapy more comfortable. This may include recognizing the importance of **family involvement**, **spiritual beliefs**, or **community support** in the healing process.
- **Demonstrating Respect for Cultural Practices:** Practitioners should take time to learn about the client's cultural practices or beliefs that might influence the therapeutic process. For example, if a client's culture includes **spiritual rituals**, the therapist might **incorporate these practices** into the E M D R process in a way that **complements** traditional E M D R techniques. In other cases, the practitioner might find it valuable to work in

collaboration with a **community leader** or **spiritual guide**.

B. Adapting Language and Metaphors

Language plays a critical role in the way we experience and understand trauma. It's important to adjust E M D R's **language-based interventions** to ensure they are culturally relevant and accessible.

- **Language Sensitivity:** In some cultures, words for emotions or psychological states may be **limited**, **nonexistent**, or understood differently. For example, there might not be an exact equivalent for terms like **depression, anxiety,** or **trauma** in certain languages. A practitioner might need to incorporate **visual metaphors, stories,** or **culturally resonant imagery** to convey therapeutic concepts.
- **Cultural Relevance of Metaphors:** E M D R uses metaphors during the **installation phase** (the phase in which positive beliefs are reinforced). When working with clients from diverse backgrounds, therapists should ensure the metaphors they use align with the **client's values**. For instance, a metaphor about **strength** in a collectivist society may emphasize **community support** and **shared responsibility**, rather than individual willpower.

C. Adjusting the E M D R Techniques

Certain techniques within the standard E M D R protocol may require adjustments to be culturally sensitive and effective:

- **Bilateral Stimulation (BLS):** The core of E M D R therapy involves the use of **Bilateral Stimulation (BLS)**, which is typically done through eye movements, tapping, or auditory tones. Depending on the client's comfort level, certain types of BLS might be more culturally appropriate than others. For example, some cultures might prefer **tactile stimulation**, such as **tapping**, rather than the **eye movement technique**.

- **Targeting the Memory Network:** While the **standard protocol** of identifying a target memory (the incident that caused the trauma) is effective across cultures, some clients may have **collective or historical traumas** that involve **group memory** (e.g., memories of **genocide**, **oppression**, or **displacement**). In such cases, the therapist may need to target both **individual experiences** and **collective memories** simultaneously.

3. Spirituality and E M D R

For clients from certain cultural or spiritual backgrounds, **spirituality** may be a core part of their healing process. Practitioners should be prepared to integrate **spiritual elements** into the E M D R process.

- **Culturally Relevant Spiritual Practices:** Some clients may feel more comfortable if spiritual practices are integrated into the therapy, such as **prayers**, **rituals**, or **affirmations**. Therapists can work collaboratively with clients to incorporate these elements in a way that complements the E M D R protocol.
- **Spiritual Support Systems:** In some cultures, **healers** or **elders** may play a critical role in the recovery process. A culturally competent therapist may choose to **collaborate** with these individuals or respect the client's preference for involving them in the healing process.

4. Addressing Cultural and Historical Trauma

In some cultural contexts, trauma is not just an individual experience but a **communal** or **societal one**. This can include issues like **colonialism**, **racism**, **displacement**, or **genocide**. These forms of trauma may impact multiple generations, and the healing process may require an approach that acknowledges the collective aspect of the pain.

- **Historical Trauma:** Practitioners can use E M D R to address **historical trauma** by helping clients process **cultural memories** or generational wounds passed down through the community. In such cases, it may be beneficial to broaden the scope of E M D R to incorporate a **multi-generational perspective**.

5. Key Strategies for Adapting E M D R to Diverse Populations

- **Respect and Validate Cultural Beliefs:** Validate and respect the client's cultural beliefs and practices. This includes **non-judgmental acceptance** of their worldview, whether it involves **family dynamics**, **spirituality**, or **community involvement**.
- **Use Culturally Relevant Language:** Adapt language and metaphors to ensure that they resonate with the client's **cultural context**. Ensure that you use terms, images, and concepts that are relevant to the client's experiences.
- **Collaborate with Community Leaders or Spiritual Guides:** In some cases, collaborating with cultural, spiritual, or community leaders can create a more supportive environment for the client.
- **Flexibility in Bilateral Stimulation:** Be flexible with BLS techniques. Some cultures may find certain methods more comfortable than others, so provide options like tapping, auditory tones, or visual cues.

Why It Stands Out: Tackles Cultural Nuances in Therapy, Offering a Unique Perspective Rarely Addressed by Competitors

One of the key differentiators of this book is its deep dive into the cultural aspects of trauma and healing, specifically tailored for **Eye Movement Desensitization and Reprocessing (E M D R)** therapy. While many E M D R guides focus primarily on the mechanics and scientific aspects of the therapy, this book **goes beyond the basics**, exploring the **cultural nuances** that shape how people from diverse backgrounds experience and heal from trauma. By integrating **cultural sensitivity** with E M D R techniques, it provides a **unique and comprehensive perspective** that is often missing in more traditional E M D R resources.

1. Recognizing the Complexity of Trauma Across Cultures

Trauma is universal in its impact, but the way it is experienced and understood can differ dramatically across cultures. This book **acknowledges these differences** and helps readers recognize that the experience of trauma cannot be fully understood without considering the **cultural context**.

- **Cultural Sensitivity in Trauma Treatment:** E M D R is often used to treat trauma related to individual events (like accidents or abuse), but for many, trauma is deeply rooted in **collective experiences** like **historical oppression, racism, displacement**, or **war.** These collective traumas shape the identity of entire communities and influence how individuals within those communities view and process personal trauma. This book introduces a framework that allows E M D R therapists to understand and address both **individual** and **cultural trauma**, making it a

broader, more inclusive approach than what is typically presented in other guides.

- **Emotional Expression Across Cultures:** The book delves into how different cultures express, process, and **cope with emotions,** providing practical strategies for adapting E M D R therapy to **culturally specific ways of emotional expression**. For example, in some cultures, emotional restraint or the avoidance of overt displays of emotion is the norm, whereas others may encourage more **outward expressions of grief or anger**. Understanding these distinctions ensures that the **therapy respects the cultural values** of the client and creates a safe space for healing.

2. Emphasizing Cultural Competence for Effective Healing

What sets this book apart from others is its **emphasis on cultural competence** in the therapeutic process. Most E M D R guides focus on the **practical steps** and **scientific theories** behind E M D R, but this book recognizes that **effective therapy requires a cultural understanding** that goes beyond techniques and theory.

- **Building Trust in Diverse Contexts:** Trust is the foundation of any therapeutic relationship, and this book explores how cultural factors can influence **rapport-building**. It offers guidance on how to build trust with clients from cultures that may be **suspicious of mental health care** or where seeking therapy is considered taboo. The book teaches how to navigate these challenges with **sensitivity** and **respect**, offering concrete strategies for connecting with clients and helping them feel heard, respected, and understood.
- **Culturally Tailored Approaches to Therapy:** Beyond general cultural awareness, this book provides readers with actionable tools to **adapt** the E M D R

process to better align with a client's **cultural beliefs**, **values**, and **social contexts**. Whether it's adjusting language, changing the way certain techniques are introduced, or incorporating cultural practices into the therapy, readers will learn how to **respectfully modify** E M D R for the unique needs of each client.

3. Highlighting Cultural Barriers to Therapy and Overcoming Them

Therapists often encounter **cultural barriers** that prevent clients from engaging in the healing process, such as **mistrust**, **fear of stigma**, or **lack of understanding** of therapy's benefits. This book **addresses these barriers head-on**, offering solutions that help readers navigate cultural differences without compromising the effectiveness of the therapy.

- **Overcoming Cultural Mistrust:** For example, many cultures have a deep mistrust of **Western mental health systems**, viewing them as **alien** or **unnatural**. This mistrust can prevent clients from feeling comfortable enough to engage with therapeutic practices like E M D R. The book provides specific strategies for overcoming these barriers, such as **working with community leaders**, **incorporating traditional healing practices**, and offering **collaborative care** that includes family or spiritual figures, allowing clients to feel **more at ease**.
- **Incorporating Spiritual Practices:** Many cultures have a strong connection to **spirituality** as part of the healing process. The book emphasizes the importance of integrating spiritual and **ritualistic practices** into E M D R when working with clients for whom these elements are significant. By blending **spirituality** with E M D R techniques, therapists can create a **holistic** healing approach that resonates

deeply with clients and enhances the therapeutic experience.

4. Providing Real-World Examples and Case Studies

To ensure that the concepts discussed are not only theoretical but also practical, the book includes **real-world case studies** from a variety of cultural backgrounds. These case studies demonstrate how E M D R can be **adapted and implemented** with clients from different cultures, and how these adaptations help overcome challenges that arise from cultural differences.

- **Examples from Diverse Backgrounds:** Case studies range from working with **immigrants and refugees** who carry the weight of **historical trauma** to **first-generation individuals** who may struggle with **cultural identity** issues. Each example is grounded in practical, **culturally tailored strategies** that can be applied to the reader's own practice.
- **Success Stories:** These stories highlight **real-life examples** of how cultural adaptation of E M D R has helped clients heal from trauma in ways that are culturally relevant and personally meaningful. Readers can learn from the **successes and challenges** faced by the practitioners in these stories, gaining insight into how they can implement these strategies in their own work.

5. Filling a Gap in the E M D R Literature

While many books on E M D R cover the **scientific foundations** of the therapy and its **step-by-step protocols**, few address the **intersection of culture and trauma**. By offering a framework that blends **E M D R's therapeutic efficacy** with **cultural competence**, this book fills a gap that many of its competitors have overlooked.

- **Beyond the Basics:** While standard E M D R guides focus primarily on the **technical aspects** of therapy—like the **eight-phase protocol**—this book emphasizes the **personal and cultural** contexts that make each client's experience of trauma unique. It highlights how culturally sensitive therapy leads to **better engagement, greater trust**, and **more successful outcomes** in the long term.
- **A More Inclusive Approach to Healing:** By tackling cultural differences in trauma and therapy, this book offers a more **inclusive approach** to E M D R, ensuring that **clients of all backgrounds** can feel **seen, heard**, and **understood**. It broadens the scope of E M D R therapy, ensuring it is not only effective but also **relevant** to a diverse population.

Chapter 15. Long-Term Healing: Life After E M D R

As individuals progress through Eye Movement Desensitization and Reprocessing (E M D R) therapy, the ultimate goal is to experience not just **temporary relief**, but **lasting healing**. While E M D R can be profoundly transformative in addressing past trauma and emotional wounds, its impact does not end with the completion of therapy. **Life after E M D R** involves integrating the healing achieved during therapy into one's daily life, continuing the journey of self-discovery, and building a future of **emotional well-being** and **resilience**. This section will explore how to maintain the progress made during E M D R and thrive in the long-term, with practical tools, strategies, and insights for sustained growth.

1. What Life After E M D R Looks Like

Life after E M D R can be described as a transition from **processing** and **healing** to **living**. While the immediate focus of E M D R is often on resolving specific trauma or emotional wounds, long-term healing involves embracing a **new way of being**—one that is **free from the weight** of past experiences, **more mindful**, and **resilient** in the face of future challenges.

- **Increased Emotional Regulation:** One of the most significant benefits of E M D R is its ability to help individuals regulate their emotions more effectively. After therapy, individuals often find themselves reacting less impulsively to stress and trauma triggers. They develop a **greater awareness of their emotional states** and can make intentional choices about how to respond to challenging situations.
- **A New Sense of Self:** For many, E M D R therapy helps them reconnect with a **stronger sense of**

identity and **self-worth**, which might have been diminished by trauma. Life after E M D R often brings about a **renewed sense of purpose** and **empowerment**. With the release of deep-seated pain, individuals may find themselves engaging in life with more **confidence**, **clarity**, and a **healthier perspective on themselves** and their potential.

2. Sustaining Emotional Wellness After E M D R

Although E M D R provides significant breakthroughs in healing trauma, it is essential for individuals to continue practicing emotional wellness after therapy. Without ongoing self-care and integration, the progress made during therapy may not be fully sustained.

- **Mindfulness and Meditation:** E M D R can make people more aware of their emotional patterns and thought processes. After therapy, incorporating **mindfulness** and **meditation** practices into one's routine can help individuals maintain emotional balance. These practices encourage a continued connection with the present moment and can aid in the prevention of **re-traumatization** or the resurfacing of old wounds.
- **Journaling and Reflection:** Many people find that **journaling** serves as a valuable tool for processing thoughts and emotions post-therapy. Regularly reflecting on emotional growth and challenges through writing can help individuals recognize **patterns of thinking** and **emotional triggers** while reinforcing the **insights** gained during E M D R.
- **Building Healthy Coping Mechanisms:** While E M D R may help resolve old patterns of unhealthy coping mechanisms, individuals must build **new, healthier habits** to deal with stress. Learning how to set boundaries, practice **self-compassion**, and use tools like **breathing exercises, grounding**

240

techniques, or **positive affirmations** ensures emotional wellness in the long term.

3. Embracing the Benefits of E M D R Long-Term

The true strength of E M D R lies in its ability to create **lasting change**. As individuals move through the stages of healing, they begin to experience the **long-term benefits** of E M D R, which continue to unfold over time.

- **Reduction in P T S D Symptoms:** For many, E M D R leads to a **long-term reduction in P T S D symptoms** like hypervigilance, nightmares, and intrusive thoughts. In the months and years following therapy, these symptoms often remain diminished, allowing individuals to experience a more peaceful, calm, and balanced life.
- **Improved Relationships:** Healing from past trauma can significantly improve one's interpersonal relationships. As individuals experience **emotional healing**, they often become better at **communicating, setting boundaries**, and **connecting** with others. Relationships that may have been strained due to unresolved trauma can evolve into healthier, more supportive dynamics.
- **Better Emotional Resilience:** E M D R helps individuals develop an **increased ability to cope with future stressors**. By addressing the root causes of trauma and emotional wounds, E M D R provides individuals with the tools to face future challenges with **greater emotional resilience**. They are less likely to be overwhelmed by setbacks or emotionally triggered by difficult situations.

4. Challenges to Expect After E M D R

While the benefits of E M D R can be profound, it is important to recognize that healing is an ongoing process.

Life after E M D R can bring new challenges, as individuals continue to grow and evolve.

- **Emotional Rebound:** After the intense emotional work done during E M D R, it's not uncommon for individuals to experience a temporary **emotional rebound**—a period where old feelings and memories may surface before they fully subside. This is often part of the **healing process**, as the brain continues to integrate the changes made during therapy. It's essential to approach this phase with **patience, self-compassion**, and **understanding** that these feelings are temporary and part of the healing journey.
- **Occasional Triggers:** While E M D R can help reduce trauma-related symptoms, **triggers** may still arise from time to time. Life after E M D R means recognizing that these triggers are not indicative of failure or regression, but an opportunity to use the **tools and strategies** learned during therapy to manage them. **Self-awareness, grounding techniques**, and **emotional regulation** can help minimize the impact of these triggers on daily life.
- **The Need for Continued Growth:** Even after E M D R therapy, it's important to recognize that healing is not a linear path. Individuals should expect that growth and personal development will continue for the rest of their lives. E M D R provides a strong foundation, but ongoing self-awareness, emotional work, and **continued therapy** (if needed) will contribute to lasting healing.

5. Moving Forward with Empowerment

In the long-term, E M D R offers individuals an opportunity to **rewrite their stories**—to move from being defined by their trauma to creating a future grounded in **empowerment, self-awareness**, and **purpose**. This final section explores the ways in which individuals can continue their journey of healing and growth beyond the confines of therapy.

- **Setting New Goals:** One of the most empowering aspects of E M D R is the ability to move past old wounds and pursue new goals. After therapy, many individuals are able to **set and achieve personal goals** that were once hindered by their trauma. Whether it's advancing in their careers, improving personal relationships, or focusing on personal growth, E M D R can free individuals from the limitations that trauma once imposed on them.
- **Becoming Advocates for Healing:** For some, life after E M D R leads to a desire to **help others**. Individuals may feel motivated to become **advocates** for mental health awareness, trauma-informed practices, or even E M D R therapists themselves. The healing they experience can inspire them to contribute to the healing of others in their communities.

What Readers Will Learn: Strategies for Maintaining Progress, Personal Growth, and Emotional Resilience After E M D R Therapy

As individuals complete their E M D R (Eye Movement Desensitization and Reprocessing) therapy, the journey does not end with the last session. Instead, **true healing** and transformation come from **maintaining progress** and continuing to nurture emotional well-being long after therapy ends. In this section, readers will learn how to apply proven **strategies** for sustaining the progress made during E M D R, promoting **personal growth**, and cultivating **emotional resilience**. These strategies are essential to ensure lasting change and long-term success in overcoming trauma and emotional wounds.

1. Cultivating Emotional Awareness

One of the first steps in maintaining progress after E M D R therapy is developing a deep, **ongoing awareness** of your emotions and reactions. **Emotional awareness** allows individuals to recognize subtle shifts in their emotional state, which is critical in preventing emotional regression or re-traumatization.

- **Daily Emotional Check-ins**: Regularly checking in with yourself throughout the day can be as simple as asking, "How am I feeling right now?" Keeping a **journal** or **emotion log** can help you track your emotional states and identify triggers or patterns that may still exist after therapy. A heightened sense of emotional awareness provides an important opportunity to **intervene early**, preventing overwhelming feelings from taking hold.
- **Mindfulness Practices**: Incorporating mindfulness techniques, such as **meditation** or **deep-breathing exercises**, helps you stay grounded in the present moment. This can reduce the emotional intensity of past trauma resurfacing unexpectedly. By being mindful of how you feel, you can better respond rather than react to challenging situations, thus ensuring long-term healing.

2. Strengthening Coping Mechanisms

During E M D R, individuals often learn new ways to manage stress, anxiety, and emotional triggers. **Strengthening** and **reinforcing** these **coping mechanisms** ensures that they remain effective long after therapy ends.

- **Building Healthy Routines**: Establishing and sticking to a healthy daily routine that includes **exercise, balanced nutrition**, and adequate **sleep** can improve mental health and help manage stress. A structured routine brings stability and balance, which can mitigate feelings of chaos or overwhelm that trauma may bring.

- **Developing Emotional Resilience Techniques**: Resilience refers to the ability to bounce back from adversity. After E M D R therapy, it's important to **continue building emotional resilience** by using tools such as **self-soothing techniques**, **grounding exercises**, and **positive self-talk**. For example, whenever you face a stressful situation, try to implement deep breathing or visualization techniques to restore a sense of calm.
- **Developing Problem-Solving Skills**: Many people who have experienced trauma often feel stuck or overwhelmed by challenges. Developing **problem-solving skills** can empower individuals to feel more in control of their circumstances, rather than overwhelmed by them. These skills include breaking down problems into manageable steps, asking for support when needed, and learning how to cope with setbacks in a healthy way.

3. Continuing Therapy or Support

While E M D R therapy is incredibly effective, emotional growth and healing are lifelong journeys. One of the most powerful strategies for maintaining progress after E M D R is to continue receiving support, either through **therapy** or **peer support**.

- **Therapy Maintenance**: Some individuals find it helpful to return to therapy for occasional **check-ins** or **booster sessions**. These sessions can help individuals stay on track, process any new challenges, or deepen their understanding of themselves. Continuing therapy, whether through **talk therapy**, **cognitive behavioral therapy (CBT)**, or other modalities, provides a consistent space for personal growth and emotional maintenance.

- **Support Groups and Peer Networks**: Being part of a **support group** or community can provide a sense of belonging and understanding, which is essential for long-term healing. Many people find strength in connecting with others who have experienced similar challenges. Whether through **online forums** or **in-person groups**, sharing experiences and advice helps reinforce progress.

4. Engaging in Ongoing Self-Care

After completing E M D R therapy, it's essential to prioritize **self-care** regularly. Taking the time to nurture your mental, emotional, and physical well-being will help keep you balanced and prevent burnout.

- **Self-Compassion Practices**: E M D R therapy can foster significant self-awareness, but maintaining **self-compassion** is key for ensuring ongoing progress. Treat yourself with kindness, especially in moments of setback. By embracing **self-compassion**, you avoid falling into negative cycles of self-blame, which can impede your healing process. Practices like **affirmations**, **self-reflection**, and engaging in things that make you feel nourished are essential parts of this process.
- **Engaging in Enjoyable Activities**: Engaging in **hobbies** or **activities that bring joy** helps build positive emotional states. Whether it's painting, reading, spending time with loved ones, or taking part in physical activities, regularly participating in things you enjoy can enhance your sense of **self-worth**, reduce stress, and keep you connected to life's simple pleasures.
- **Rest and Recharging**: Healing takes energy, and rest is crucial. Scheduling regular **time for rest**, relaxation, and reflection helps prevent burnout and restores emotional and physical vitality. This might include **weekends off**, **mindful breaks**, or simply

making sure to **get enough sleep** to support long-term healing.

5. Setting and Achieving New Goals

Post-E M D R is an excellent time to look forward and **set new goals**. With the emotional weight of trauma lifted, individuals often feel a **new sense of possibility** and can pursue personal, professional, or relational goals with renewed enthusiasm.

- **Small, Achievable Goals**: Start with **small, manageable goals** that support your growth and keep you focused on the future. Whether it's building a new skill, exploring a creative outlet, or setting boundaries in relationships, goal-setting allows you to see and celebrate your progress.
- **Reflecting on Values and Priorities**: Reflecting on your core values and how they align with your long-term goals can help clarify your next steps. E M D R therapy often uncovers deep insights about your inner needs and desires. Take the time to **define** and **align your actions** with your personal values. This ensures that your journey of healing and growth continues in a meaningful direction.

6. Dealing with Setbacks Gracefully

Life will inevitably present challenges, and emotional setbacks may arise. Learning how to **manage setbacks gracefully** without losing confidence in the progress made during E M D R is a crucial aspect of long-term healing.

- **Normalizing Setbacks**: Understand that setbacks are part of the healing journey and do not represent failure. **Resilience** is not about avoiding obstacles; it's about how you bounce back from them. Practice **self-compassion** during difficult moments, and remember that healing is non-linear.

- **Reaching Out for Support**: If setbacks feel overwhelming, don't hesitate to seek additional support. Whether it's reconnecting with your therapist, a trusted friend, or a support group, reaching out can help you regain perspective and motivation. **Connection** and **support** are powerful tools for overcoming challenges.

7. Celebrating Progress and Growth

It's essential to regularly take time to **celebrate** the progress you've made. Acknowledging your own resilience and growth helps reinforce your continued healing.

- **Track Milestones**: Keep track of your healing milestones, no matter how small they may seem. Whether it's improved emotional regulation, healthier relationships, or a new sense of personal empowerment, recognizing these milestones keeps you motivated and connected to your journey.
- **Celebrate Your Strength**: Recognize your inner strength and the courage it took to work through trauma. By celebrating your ability to heal, you reinforce your sense of **empowerment** and **self-worth**, ensuring that you continue to thrive beyond therapy.

Why It Stands Out: Focuses on Life Beyond Therapy, Offering Readers Tools for Long-Term Success

What truly sets this book apart is its emphasis on **life beyond therapy**, recognizing that healing does not conclude once the final E M D R session is over. While E M D R therapy is a transformative process, the journey toward emotional resilience and personal growth is ongoing. This book not only guides readers through the **healing process** but also equips them with **practical tools** to ensure **lasting success**. By offering resources for **long-term emotional**

well-being, it provides readers with the means to continue growing and thriving long after their therapy sessions have ended.

Here's why this approach is so important:

1. Emphasizing Lifelong Healing and Personal Growth

Healing from trauma is not a finite event; it is a **continuous process** that evolves over time. While E M D R is an incredibly effective technique for processing trauma, true **lasting change** comes from integrating the lessons learned in therapy into **everyday life**. This book places significant focus on the **lifelong journey of emotional growth**, showing that once the heavy lifting of trauma processing is done, there is still much to be explored in terms of personal development.

- **Self-Discovery Beyond Trauma**: The book encourages readers to move beyond just surviving trauma to truly living. It offers strategies for pursuing **personal growth**—whether that means exploring new passions, setting long-term goals, or deepening interpersonal relationships. The focus shifts from just "healing" to **thriving** in a way that embraces the full range of human potential.
- **Emotional Resilience for the Future**: Building resilience is not just about recovering from past wounds but preparing for life's inevitable challenges. This book prepares readers for a future where they are equipped to handle stress, grief, disappointment, and change with a **resilient mindset**. It emphasizes the importance of developing skills that will serve them not only in times of crisis but also in daily interactions, helping them bounce back stronger each time life throws curveballs.

2. Equipping Readers with Tools for Self-Sufficiency

While therapy is transformative, the real power comes from developing the **self-sufficiency** to continue the healing process outside the therapist's office. This book offers readers a **toolbox** of exercises, techniques, and **self-guided practices** that can be used long after the therapeutic process. It empowers readers to take control of their healing and emotional health, fostering an ongoing sense of ownership over their personal journey.

- **Practical Self-Care Strategies**: The book highlights the importance of **daily self-care**—not just in the context of therapy but as an essential part of maintaining emotional health long-term. It provides clear, actionable steps for integrating **mindfulness**, **breathing exercises**, **journaling**, and other self-care techniques into everyday life. This approach ensures that readers have accessible tools to keep their emotions in balance as they continue their healing journey.
- **Strengthening Emotional Awareness**: One of the keys to long-term success is the ability to stay connected to your **emotional landscape**. This book helps readers develop skills to notice, track, and manage their emotional states. By encouraging regular emotional check-ins and offering practical strategies to **process difficult emotions** in real-time, it ensures that readers will always have a way to maintain emotional balance and avoid stagnation.

3. Long-Term Healing, Not Just Short-Term Fixes

Many trauma recovery resources focus solely on **quick fixes** or immediate relief from symptoms. While short-term results are important, this book takes a deeper, more holistic approach. It focuses on **long-term healing**, giving readers the tools to ensure they continue to grow emotionally and mentally long after their therapy concludes.

- **Building Sustainable Healing Practices**: The book teaches readers how to create a **healing routine** that lasts, with practices they can use every day to support their emotional well-being. From **meditative practices** to **healthy boundaries**, it gives readers the framework they need to stay grounded and supported over the long haul.
- **Creating a Personal Recovery Plan**: The book emphasizes the importance of creating a **personalized recovery plan** that goes beyond therapy. This includes setting **long-term emotional goals**, mapping out **wellness practices**, and regularly reassessing progress. By teaching readers to tailor their recovery to their own needs, it ensures that they are prepared for whatever life throws at them.

4. Integrating Life Lessons from E M D R into Daily Life

Through E M D R therapy, many people uncover profound insights into their emotional patterns, core beliefs, and reactions. The **real challenge** comes in integrating these insights into daily life in a way that leads to sustained emotional balance and well-being. This book focuses on **practical integration**, offering readers tools and strategies to turn their E M D R lessons into **daily habits** and **life principles**.

- **Integrating E M D R Insights**: Rather than simply processing trauma during therapy and moving on, this book focuses on how to **embed the lessons** learned during E M D R into everyday life. It offers tips on how to integrate **new beliefs, healthy coping strategies**, and **boundary-setting skills** into relationships, work, and personal growth. This seamless integration ensures that the changes made in therapy are not just temporary but a permanent shift toward healthier patterns of living.

- **Turning Insights into Action**: Insights gained from E M D R therapy are only as effective as the action taken to apply them. This book offers actionable steps for turning **aha moments** into **life-changing decisions**. It explores how to implement **new ways of thinking** and **behaving** that are aligned with the healing process, empowering readers to continue evolving beyond therapy.

5. Encouraging a Holistic Approach to Recovery

This book takes a **holistic approach** to recovery, acknowledging that healing involves more than just emotional work—it requires attention to every aspect of a person's well-being, including the physical, mental, and spiritual components. By addressing all of these areas, it ensures readers are supported in **creating a well-rounded** and **sustainable** healing practice that lasts long into the future.

- **Physical Health and Emotional Healing**: The connection between body and mind is explored in-depth, with tips on maintaining **physical health** to support emotional well-being. The book encourages regular exercise, proper nutrition, and sleep, which are all crucial to managing stress and trauma recovery. The importance of **self-compassion** is also emphasized to ensure that readers nurture themselves holistically.
- **Mental Clarity and Self-Reflection**: The book encourages readers to **engage in reflective practices** that promote ongoing mental clarity. Techniques like **journaling, meditation**, and **mindfulness** allow individuals to maintain emotional balance, enhance their self-awareness, and remain focused on their healing journey long after therapy has ended.

6. Offering Ongoing Support Through the Healing Process

Recognizing that trauma recovery does not occur in isolation, this book offers a **community of support**. It not only offers tools for the individual but also acknowledges the importance of ongoing **connection with others** in the healing journey.

- **Support Networks**: The book encourages readers to **seek out supportive communities**—whether through **therapy groups**, **online forums**, or **peer support networks**. This sense of belonging and connection ensures that individuals never feel alone on their healing journey and are always able to access guidance and compassion when needed.
- **Accountability and Encouragement**: Long-term success in trauma recovery often requires **accountability**. This book provides guidance on finding an **accountability partner** or support group to help maintain progress and keep you motivated. With ongoing encouragement, readers are more likely to stick to their recovery plans and continue working toward long-term emotional health.

Conclusion

A Journey of Healing and Empowerment

As we reach the end of this guide to **E M D R therapy** and emotional healing, it is important to reflect on the remarkable journey that you, the reader, have embarked upon. Whether you're someone seeking relief from trauma, anxiety, or emotional wounds, or you are looking to enhance your self-healing practices, this book has aimed to provide you with the **knowledge, tools**, and **strategies** necessary for profound healing and growth.

Throughout these chapters, we've explored the science behind E M D R therapy, the process itself, the potential for self-help applications, and how it can address various forms of trauma. But more importantly, we've placed a strong emphasis on **life beyond therapy**—focusing on **long-term emotional well-being, personal growth**, and the **empowerment** that comes with taking ownership of your healing journey. The path to emotional resilience does not end with the completion of therapy; it is a lifelong commitment to growth, understanding, and healing.

Your Healing Journey Is Just Beginning

You've now been introduced to a therapeutic method that has helped countless individuals heal from deeply rooted emotional wounds. By the time you've completed your E M D R sessions—or even as you continue to engage with some of the **self-help techniques** outlined in this book—you will have gained invaluable insights into the ways that **trauma** has shaped your life and the steps you can take to shift your emotional and psychological patterns. But this journey is not an end, it's a **new beginning**.

The **tools** and **self-help strategies** in this book are designed to **complement** and **enhance** the transformative power of E M D R therapy. They are **practical, actionable**, and grounded in real-world experience. By incorporating these practices into your everyday life, you will find that emotional healing is not something that happens overnight but rather a process of **consistent, mindful practice**.

Sustaining Progress Through Lifelong Growth

What sets this guide apart is its focus on **long-term success**. It goes beyond the **immediate relief** of symptoms and instead works to instill **lifelong practices** that promote **sustained well-being**. This is not just about managing symptoms but about developing an ongoing relationship with yourself—one in which you remain committed to nurturing your **mental health, emotional resilience**, and **personal growth**.

By leveraging the **insights gained from E M D R** and continuously integrating them into your life, you arc actively shaping a future that is **freer, healthier**, and more **empowered**. Healing doesn't have a finish line—it's about moving forward in a way that honors the work you've already done and celebrates the progress you continue to make.

Your Tools for Ongoing Healing

As you move forward, keep in mind that **healing** is not linear, and there will be times when you face setbacks or challenges. The beauty of this process is in learning how to **navigate those moments** with the skills you have gained—whether it's through **mindfulness, journaling, self-care practices**, or seeking out the support of others. It's also essential to recognize that healing is a **personal journey**—there's no one right way to go about it. The **tools** provided here are just a starting point for discovering what works best for you, enabling you to **customize your recovery plan** in a way that feels authentic and empowering.

Embracing the Future with Confidence

As you conclude this guide, remember that you are **not alone** in your healing journey. Whether you are navigating the effects of **trauma, anxiety,** or **emotional wounds**, you are part of a larger community of individuals who have found strength, healing, and transformation through E M D R therapy. And as you integrate these principles into your life, you can be confident that you are **taking steps toward emotional freedom**—one that will support you as you **create the life you deserve**.

The principles of **E M D R** are not just limited to the therapy room; they are tools for **life**—tools for navigating challenges, maintaining emotional balance, and fostering **personal growth**. As you continue your journey, trust in the process, stay committed to your healing, and know that the future holds immense possibilities for personal and emotional fulfillment.

A Final Note

The road ahead may seem uncertain, and you may encounter moments of doubt or difficulty. But remember, the journey you have started is one of **growth, empowerment**, and **resilience**. You have the ability to overcome your past, transform your present, and shape your future. E M D R therapy has already set you on the path to healing, but it's the work you do every day—through the insights you gain and the practices you incorporate—that will ensure you continue to thrive.

Take a moment to reflect on the strength it took to get this far. Now, embrace the healing that lies ahead and the incredible power you possess to transform your emotional well-being and your life.

You are more than your trauma. You are capable of deep healing, profound emotional freedom, and a life filled with growth, love, and **resilience**.

Thank you for trusting this guide to accompany you on your journey. Wishing you peace, healing, and empowerment every step of the way.

References

Below is a list of references consulted and cited throughout this book. These resources provide further depth and evidence to the principles, practices, and science of E M D R therapy, trauma healing, and emotional resilience.

Books and Journals

1. **Shapiro, F.** (2017). *Eye Movement Desensitization and Reprocessing (E M D R) Therapy: Basic Principles, Protocols, and Procedures* (3rd ed.). New York: Guilford Press.
This foundational text by Francine Shapiro, the developer of E M D R, provides an in-depth look at the science behind E M D R, its clinical protocols, and practical applications for trauma healing.

2. **Hase, M., & Goldsmith, S.** (2015). *E M D R in the Treatment of Adults Abused as Children: A Case Study Approach.* New York: Springer Publishing.
This book offers case studies that demonstrate the effectiveness of E M D R therapy in treating complex trauma and childhood abuse.

3. **Van der Kolk, B. A.** (2014). *The Body Keeps the Score: Brain, Mind, and Body in the Healing of Trauma.* New York: Viking.
Dr. Bessel van der Kolk's seminal work explores how trauma affects the body and the brain, and discusses innovative therapies, including E M D R, for trauma recovery.

4. **Shapiro, F., & Laliotis, D.** (2011). *E M D R and the Art of Psychotherapy with Children: Infants to Adolescents.* New York: Guilford Press.
This comprehensive guide delves into how E M D R can be adapted for children and adolescents, offering insights into trauma healing for younger populations.

5. **Spring, J. A.** (2007). *E M D R: The Breakthrough Therapy for Overcoming Anxiety, Stress, and Trauma.* New York: Plume.

A practical guide to understanding E M D R's applications in treating a wide range of emotional issues, including stress, anxiety, and P T S D.

Articles and Studies

6. **Shapiro, F.** (2001). "Eye Movement Desensitization and Reprocessing (E M D R) in the Treatment of Trauma." *Journal of Clinical Psychology*, 57(3), 299-313.
   This article presents the foundational research supporting E M D R therapy's effectiveness in trauma treatment, examining its application and efficacy.
7. **Carlson, J. G., & Chemtob, C. M.** (2004). "E M D R in the Treatment of Post-Traumatic Stress Disorder." *Journal of Clinical Psychology*, 60(7), 1081-1092.
   This study explores the clinical outcomes of E M D R therapy in individuals diagnosed with P T S D, highlighting its impact on trauma processing.
8. **Maxfield, L., & Hyer, L. A.** (2002). "E M D R Treatment of Combat Veterans with Post-Traumatic Stress Disorder." *Journal of Clinical Psychology*, 58(1), 37-46.
   This article discusses the application of E M D R therapy with combat veterans suffering from P T S D, providing evidence of its success in military settings.
9. **Marr, M. G.** (2006). "Trauma and the Brain: An Overview of Current Neuroscientific Findings." *Neuropsychology Review*, 16(1), 35-43.
   This article explains the neurobiological mechanisms behind trauma and healing, offering a neuroscience perspective that aligns with the E M D R approach.

Websites and Online Resources

10. **E M D R International Association (E M D RIA).** (2021). "What is E M D R?" Retrieved from www.e m d ria.org

E M D RIA is the leading organization for E M D R therapists and offers a wealth of resources about E M D R therapy, including evidence-based research, training, and practitioner directories.

11. **The Trauma Foundation.** (2020). "Understanding Trauma and Its Impact on the Brain." Retrieved from www.traumafoundation.org
    This nonprofit provides valuable resources on trauma recovery, including understanding its effects on the brain and how therapies like E M D R can aid in recovery.

12. **National Institute of Mental Health (NIMH).** (2019). "Post-Traumatic Stress Disorder (P T S D)." Retrieved from www.nimh.nih.gov
    The NIMH provides extensive information about P T S D, its causes, symptoms, and treatments, including the use of E M D R in trauma therapy.

Other Key References

13. **Leeds, A. M.** (2009). *A Guide to E M D R: The Basics and Beyond.* New York: Norton & Company.
    A practical and user-friendly guide to E M D R, aimed at both therapists and those interested in using E M D R for self-help and healing.

14. **Franklin, C. L., & Zeanah, C. H.** (2017). "Attachment and Trauma: A Neurodevelopmental Approach to Treatment." *Development and Psychopathology*, 29(3), 973-993.
    This paper examines how attachment styles interact with trauma and the neurodevelopmental effects of early life trauma, providing context for the importance of therapy like E M D R.

Author Name

Dr. Natalie Anderson is a renowned psychologist and trauma therapist with over 15 years of experience in the field of mental health. Holding a doctorate in Clinical Psychology from Stanford University, she specializes in trauma recovery and the application of innovative therapeutic techniques such as E M D R (Eye Movement Desensitization and Reprocessing). Throughout her career, Dr. Anderson has worked with a diverse range of clients, including individuals suffering from P T S D, anxiety, depression, and childhood trauma.

Her passion for healing trauma stems from her personal experience as a survivor of a traumatic event in her early adulthood. This journey sparked a deep interest in therapeutic modalities that could foster long-term recovery and emotional well-being. After being introduced to E M D R therapy during her doctoral studies, Dr. Anderson became a certified E M D R therapist and later a trainer, guiding other professionals in mastering this powerful technique.

Dr. Anderson is also the author of several scholarly articles on trauma and recovery and has been featured in numerous publications, including *Psychology Today* and *The Journal of Trauma and Recovery*. In addition to her clinical work, she conducts workshops and seminars on trauma healing, E M D R therapy, and mindfulness practices, helping individuals and mental health professionals alike.

With a warm, empathetic approach, Dr. Anderson is committed to empowering others through self-help tools, providing a holistic view of trauma recovery. In her free time, she enjoys hiking, practicing yoga, and spending time with her family.

Dr. Anderson's goal in writing this book is to make E M D R therapy accessible to anyone seeking to heal emotional wounds, regardless of whether they are receiving formal therapy or practicing techniques on their own.

Disclaimer:

The information presented in this book is for educational and informational purposes only and is not intended as professional advice. The author and publisher have made every effort to ensure the accuracy of the information; however, they assume no responsibility for errors, omissions, or any outcomes resulting from the application of the contents. Readers are encouraged to consult with a qualified professional for specific advice tailored to their situation.

All opinions expressed are those of the author and do not reflect the views of any affiliated organizations. The reader assumes all risks for the use of the material provided in this book. The author and publisher disclaim any liability for direct or indirect consequences arising from the use or interpretation of the information.

Copyright

Legal Notice

This book is for informational and educational purposes only. While the author and publisher have made every effort to provide accurate and up-to-date information, they assume no responsibility for any errors, inaccuracies, or omissions. Any reliance placed on the information in this book is strictly at the reader's discretion and risk.

The content is not intended to replace professional advice, including but not limited to medical, legal, financial, or other professional services. Readers should consult with an appropriate professional for specific guidance related to their unique circumstances.

All trademarks, product names, and company names mentioned herein are the property of their respective owners. Their inclusion does not imply endorsement, affiliation, or sponsorship. Unauthorized reproduction, distribution, or transmission of this publication in any form is prohibited without prior written consent from the author or publisher.

By reading this book, you agree to indemnify and hold harmless the author, publisher, and any affiliated parties from and against all claims, liabilities, losses, or damages resulting from your use of the information provided.

Acknowledgements

Writing this book has been an incredibly rewarding journey, and I am deeply grateful to all those who have contributed to its creation and supported me along the way.

First, I want to express my heartfelt gratitude to the brave individuals who shared their personal stories with me. Your experiences of healing and transformation through E M D R have not only inspired this book but also affirmed the power of this therapeutic method in addressing deep emotional wounds. Your courage and vulnerability are truly remarkable.

I would like to thank my mentors and colleagues in the field of psychology, particularly those who have trained and inspired me in the practice of E M D R. Your guidance, expertise, and unwavering dedication to trauma recovery have shaped my professional journey and influenced the content of this book.

To my family, thank you for your continuous love and support. Your belief in me has been a constant source of motivation, especially during the challenging moments of writing and research. I am forever grateful for your patience and understanding.

To my editor and publishing team, thank you for your expertise and meticulous attention to detail. Your feedback has been invaluable in ensuring that this book is clear, accessible, and effective in helping others on their healing journey. Your professionalism and commitment have been beyond exceptional.

Finally, to the countless individuals who are on the path of healing, this book is for you. It is my hope that the information and tools shared here empower you to take the next step toward emotional well-being, whether you are seeking professional help or exploring self-help techniques. Healing is possible, and you are never alone on this journey.

With deepest gratitude and respect,
Dr. Natalie Anderson

www.ingramcontent.com/pod-product-compliance
Lightning Source LLC
Chambersburg PA
CBHW061032250726
48653CB00001B/58